To: Kaye and Vreni, for their help

Edited by: Vreni Merriam and Marsha Weese

Published by University Book Store Press
Printed on the Espresso Book Machine
4326 University Way NE
Seattle, WA 98105
www.ubookstore.com

ISBN: 978-1-937358-22-8

FIRST SHIP
by John Merriam

I ran away from my New England home when I was 15. That's a long story. An aunt and uncle who lived near Seattle took me in until I finished high school. When I graduated in 1969 Boeing had just gone bust, laying off thousands of workers, and there were no jobs in the Seattle area. I got a summer employment guide and started sending out applications. I might just as well have been throwing darts at a map of the United States. One of the places that accepted me was a resort hotel on the coast of Maine. I had enough money saved from part-time jobs for airfare to Boston, and hitchhiked to Maine from there.

Newagen Inn is on a rocky cape that juts into the Atlantic Ocean north of Portland and just south of Boothbay Harbor. For July and August I was the Houseboy, dealing with laundry and helping the chambermaids get linen and other supplies. It was a fun summer, even though the pay was only $150/month plus whatever tips the chambermaids were willing to share.

In 1969 marijuana and LSD were everywhere on the West Coast. Those drugs were a lot harder to come by in the rest of the country, including the coast of Maine. That was part of the reason why the Maine State Police were very interested when one of the dishwashers at Newagen Inn had a bad trip and flipped out. He was a young guy from Maine, slightly retarded, and told the detective that he bought the acid he took from a waiter in the dining room named Phillip. Phillip told the detective that he'd gotten the LSD from me. Then I got interviewed by the detective. The detective was convinced that I was the source of the LSD and that I'd gotten it from some pushers he was after in Portland. He said he'd make a deal with me, letting me off the hook if I would identify my supplier. I didn't admit to anything but showed some interest in his offer, and said I needed some time to think about it. It was near the end of the season, and what I was really doing was buying time to get the hell out of Maine. My original plan, after the summer job was over, was to hitchhike to upstate New York, where I'd heard there was to be a big rock festival at Woodstock. I blew off Woodstock and fled to Seattle instead.

There was still no work in the Seattle area. I answered an ad by American Encyclopedia Co. for a career opportunity. It was basically a door-to-door sales hustle for outrageously-priced encyclopedia sets that were supposed to turn kids into geniuses. I lasted through three days of training and two hours on the job. The training consisted of memorization and rote recitation of a long sales pitch. Everyone in south Seattle slammed the door in my face that first day out, and I couldn't even start the supposedly irresistible come-on about why these people really needed an expensive set of encyclopedias. Finally a younger woman was kind enough to let me into her apartment. I was about five minutes into the canned spiel when she started reciting it ahead of me, saying the words I was going to say before I said them! So much for having an "exclusive sales presentation." The nice woman said she felt sorry for me. She obviously had felt sorry for other encyclopedia salesmen with the exact same pitch. I took my sales briefcase with samples in it back to the company and quit. American Encyclopedia Co. said I owed them $75 for the training sessions and use of the briefcase. "Sue me!" I said as I walked out.

In early October I got a minimum wage job—$1.60/hour—at Arby's, a wanna-be-McDonald's roast beef sandwich joint in Bellevue, across Lake Washington from Seattle. The owner of the franchise was Wally Rosen, a roly-poly guy from Chicago. Wally liked that I was a hard worker but it really pissed him off that I ate so much food on the job. Part of the pay was eating there during our meal break. I turned 18 that September and was still growing. In 30 minutes, every day during my break, I put down three large Arby's sandwiches and three half-pints of milk.

As soon as I turned 18 I got classified I-A by my draft board, Local Board #6, located in Room 1136 at the Federal Office Building on 1st Avenue downtown. I didn't worry too much about getting sent to Viet Nam, not then anyway, because I started sucking up to an elderly spinster on the draft board called Miss Craig. She thought I was a nice, polite boy. There was a large pool of other young men who could be used for cannon-fodder in Asia, it seemed to me. The draft board was going after people who made a lot of noise—like members of the SDS (Students for a Democratic Society) and YIP (Youth International Party —Yippies). Anyway, I had bigger concerns than the draft, like going to prison in Maine.

In October I telephoned the Maine detective who'd interviewed me. I told him that I hadn't decided yet whether or not to make a deal. He said that he was tired of waiting and that I could tell a prosecutor what I'd decided. "Are you coming to get me?" The detective knew I lived in Seattle.

"Yes."

"When?"

"As soon as our budget allows for a round-trip to the West Coast."

"I'm not guilty." I hung up before he could trace my call.

I needed to change my identity and get out of town! It was easy to get a social security number and a library card in a phony name. With that identification, it was even easier to get a draft card. A lot of young guys were publicly burning their draft cards at the time and no one in the Selective Service System would even dream that someone would register for the draft if he didn't have to. To change my appearance, all I did was get a haircut. Back then, switching from a long-hair to a clean-cut member of the silent majority was a disguise by itself. I didn't bother getting a fake driver's license because I didn't have a car. That could wait until later, if I needed it, at wherever I ended up.

In early November 1969 I gave notice that I was quitting Arby's. Wally asked me to stay, offering to make me Assistant Manager at $1.85/hour. I guess he'd gotten over his anger about the three roast beef sandwiches going down my gullet every day. I told him I had to move on.

I'm not sure why I chose to hide out in New Orleans. I didn't have any friends or relatives who lived there, and didn't know anybody who'd even been to that part of the South. I'd recently seen the movie "Easy Rider." Peter Fonda and Dennis Hopper seemed to have a good time in New Orleans, and perhaps I could too…? Or maybe I thought that would be the last place the Maine detective would look for me. I used most of my Arby's savings for a plane ticket.

I arrived in New Orleans on November 6, 1969 with $40 in my wallet. I got a room at the YMCA and went looking for a job. I found one quickly, close by at 1304 St. Charles Street, and went to work the next day.

Novelty Vendors stabled maybe 25 hot dog carts in a small, high-ceilinged warehouse. They were deployed in the French Quarter every night to sell chili dogs to drunken tourists and sports fans at an inflated price. I got hired with no questions asked. The job started each day with chopping onions to put on the chili dogs. Then we donned a red-and-white striped coat and a paper hat, before pushing our carts to various locations in the French Quarter and on Canal Street. The carts themselves were false advertising, consisting of a metal bun containing two chili dogs in it, instead of the single dog one actually received. That was perversely appropriate because each chili dog cost 45 cents, about double the price one would pay anywhere else. My pay was 11 cents out of each 45-cent chili dog sold.

In addition to how rapidly one could push a hot dog cart to the French Quarter, there was a seniority system of sorts about who would get which intersection to hawk chili dogs from. We set out at 5:00 in the afternoon and worked until most of the tourists had burned out or passed out from partying—straggling back to the stable usually just before dawn. On the first night, as the new guy, I ended up parking my cart on Decatur Street—far from the action on Bourbon Street. I was pegged for a Yankee as soon as I opened my mouth to potential customers. "Where ya from—New York?" was a typical comment. Thanks to my multi-lingual Swiss mother I'm good at accents and quickly honed what I thought sounded like a cross between speech from natives of Alabama and Georgia. That served to stop tourists from spotting me as a Northerner, but was vague enough to also prevent any customer from wanting to commiserate as a neighbor and spot me for a fraud. I sold only about 30 chili dogs in 12 hours. Even with tips I made less than $5 that night.

Selling chili dogs was pretty much one's last chance to make an honest living in New Orleans. The owner of Novelty Vendors was a little shylock with a pock-marked face named Steve. Steve rode around on a three-wheeled Harley-Davidson to keep an eye on us. He wasn't always successful. I didn't see it happen, but rumor had it that one of the vendors said "Fuck Steve!" took off his hat and striped jacket, and tossed them on the ground. Then he walked his chili dog cart to the end of Canal and pushed it into the Mississippi River.

There was a high turnover at Novelty Vendors and by the third night I had enough seniority to work Bourbon Street. I got an eyeful watching hustlers, hookers and pimps throughout the night. Tourists and sports fans came from all over the South to get drunk and act stupid. They asked me dumb questions and I'd give them snappy comebacks in my newly-adopted southern accent. Sometimes women would come on to me, while standing right next to their husbands or boyfriends. Selling chili dogs in the French Quarter was not boring! But even on a good night I made less than $15.

The employment situation in New Orleans was a lot better than it was in Seattle, though. I looked around for a better job in the afternoons before going into the stable to chop onions. After about a week of hawking chili dogs, I went to some sort of job center run by the state, took an aptitude test, and quickly landed a factory job across the river in Gretna, Louisiana.

The Wesson Oil plant on 4th Street in Gretna was a union shop and I was paid $2.48/hour—$2.58 when on second shift (4:00 to midnight), every other week. That was the most money I'd ever made. I moved out of the Y and got a studio apartment in the French Quarter for $70/month—with a small refrigerator, two stove burners and no telephone. It was on the second floor at 1130 Dauphine Street, between Urselines and Gov. Nicholls. About six units surrounded a small courtyard, accessible through a locked cast-iron gate. Every day I walked to Canal Street, caught the streetcar at St. Charles to Jackson Avenue, and then took the bus on Jackson to the Mississippi. From the foot of Jackson I caught a ferry across the river to Gretna. I can't remember if I caught another bus to the factory from there. I think I walked.

Out of maybe 50 employees at the Wesson oil factory—all male— the only other whites were a couple of homosexuals who pretty much kept to themselves. In addition to being a white boy, I was also the new guy and was given the worst job in the factory. It consisted of being at the very start of the production line on the second floor, upending boxes containing empty glass bottles of Wesson Oil and placing them on the conveyor belt. A forklift driver delivered the boxes by pallet-load, each box containing 12 empty bottles. The bottles in the boxes were neck down, so by inverting the boxes and slapping the contents onto the conveyor belt, the bottles were in an upright position, ready to descend to the first floor where they'd be filled with oil by automatic spouts. After being filled to an exact level, each bottle proceeded along the conveyor belt to be capped and labeled. Then the bottles traveled past the guy on quality control, who was supposed to look for defects, and got put back into the boxes of 12 each. The assembly line ended after the boxes were sealed. At that point the boxes were manually stacked onto pallets. Another forklift driver picked up the full pallets and took them to the warehouse, to be later put into trucks at the loading dock.

The reason my job was the worst was because of the never-ending demand to place empty bottles on the conveyor belt—fast—emptying one box after another at a maddening pace, over and over and over. After four hours the conveyor belt stopped 30 minutes for the lunch break. Other than that, the belt was a ceaseless taskmaster and never stopped. The only exception was during rare mechanical problems. During one mechanical breakdown I was biding my time on the second floor when I spotted a small green lizard scurrying out from underneath a pallet of boxes. I caught the lizard and dropped it into one of the empty bottles of Wesson Oil. When the belt started up again I watched as the bottle containing my lizard got filled, capped and labeled, and then sailed past the guy daydreaming on quality control. I kept watching as the bottle was boxed and taken to the warehouse for shipment. I should have felt remorse—not for the lizard but about the reaction of some poor housewife who probably would put that bottle of Wesson Oil into her shopping cart without taking a good look before she brought it home—but I didn't. I thought it was funny.

After 30 days of proving that I could keep up with feeding the conveyor belt, I graduated from my probationary period and was assured of a job through the Meat Cutters union, which had organized the factory. It also meant I had to join the union—officially called the Amalgamated Meat Cutters and Butcher Workmen of North America.

"Sign here." The shop steward, a burly guy, came up to me during a lunch break. By then I'd been working at easier locations on the belt. My assignment that day was quality control. Watching identical bottles go by at the rate of perhaps 150 per minute soon became one's own TV show, an invitation to hallucination. I understood how my lizard had sailed past the guy on quality control before.

"Sign what?" I didn't like being told what to do by strangers.

"You're joining the Union." The guy moved closer in an intimidating manner.

"What if I don't want to join?" I would later recognize unions as a far lesser evil than the abuses that some employers tried to get away with. At the time, however, I was young and rebellious with little experience.

"You'll get fired." I didn't know that Louisiana had closed shop laws, let alone what that even meant. For union workplaces, joining the union was a condition of keeping one's job.

I asked a few more questions, thought about my chili-dog cart, and signed reluctantly. I retained resentment about being forced to join anything I didn't want to, to say nothing of the $33 initiation fee.

I was lonely in New Orleans. I didn't have anyone to spend time with, outside of the 40 hours/week I worked at the plant in Gretna. I'd drink fortified wine and raise hell with some of the young guys at the factory, after we got off on Fridays, but didn't have much company the rest of the time. I was a Yankee with a phony accent and a phony name.

For Thanksgiving I treated myself to a meal at a fancy restaurant on Royal Street, trying to pretend I was somebody important. I dreaded the thought of spending Christmas alone.

As it happened, I got notified that I was to be laid off from the factory just before Christmas until after New Year's due to lack of work. That made me even more depressed about the upcoming holidays.

The Wesson Oil plant was part of a large Hunt-Wesson factory yard that included another plant for Snowdrift shortening. There was an industrial siding of railroad tracks on the grounds of the factory where the Snowdrift was delivered—in liquid form when slightly heated—by tank car. On December 23rd there was a massive spill of vegetable oil from a tank car, which solidified into a carpet of white shortening several inches deep. A guy named Booker was supposed to be in control of transferring the liquid Snowdrift from the tank car to holding tanks but he fell asleep during the process, letting one of the holding tanks overflow. Rumor had it that the security guard who woke Booker up found an empty pint of Ten High bourbon on the floor next to Booker's feet.

On December 24th I was laid off at the Wesson Oil plant and re-hired immediately, to clean up after Booker, by the Snowdrift division of Hunt-Wesson, Inc. I never missed a day of work. The factory yard looked like my New Hampshire home that Christmas Eve, covered in white, and it quelled my homesickness in an odd way. Never mind that

I was shoveling "snow" as heavy as lard while it was 70 degrees outside, in 90% humidity. Together with some of my pals from the Wesson Oil line, we filled maybe 200 55-gallon drums with shortening.

Booker was fired. It took until just after New Year's to shovel up all the shortening, just when the Wesson Oil line started up again and I went back to my previous job. Again, I didn't miss a day of work.

I was pathologically frugal while working for Hunt-Wesson and put about 50% of my gross wages into a savings account at Whitney National Bank. I didn't know what was going to happen next in my life and figured I needed to have as much money as possible in case I had to flee again. I telephoned the Maine detective every month or two— making quick calls from phone booths so he couldn't trace my location —to check on his intentions. He kept making excuses about budgetary problems but said that, sooner or later, he was coming for me. I began to wonder if the detective was bullshitting me. "He doesn't know where I am," I thought. "Even if he did, all he's got for evidence is the say-so of Phillip, that little fink from Newagen Inn. How will he get a conviction?" I started loosening up a bit and allowing myself some small pleasures. One was to go to an oyster bar for a late lunch on those days when I was working second shift. It felt pretty good to wash down half-a-dozen small oysters on the half-shell with a Dixie beer before going to work. Another was to go to the Seven Seas Bar—I think it was on Chartres Street. I was still 18. Shortly after I arrived in New Orleans, I'd asked a bartender how old one had to be to drink alcohol in Louisiana. "In the Quarter," he replied, "the drinking age is being tall enough to reach the bar."

I was too cheap to order more than a single beer each night I was at the Seven Seas. I mostly went there to play chess and get some companionship with people who wouldn't ask too many questions about my background. Next door there was a kitchen-restaurant-type of joint that sold huge plates of red beans and rice for 35 cents. Some of the men I played chess with were merchant seamen. We'd get to talking between moves and they'd tell me tall tales about foreign ports and how much money they made. One of them showed me his seaman's papers, a Merchant Mariner's Document, the identification card that allowed him to work aboard ships. On the front was the man's photograph, name and address, date of birth and citizenship. Also stamped across the front in large red letters was: Valid for Emergency Service Only. On the back of the card were the man's description, fingerprint, date and place of issuance for the Document, and the ratings for which he was qualified to work aboard ships.

"What does "Emergency Service" mean," I asked.

"It means I can only be drafted in a national emergency, like World War II." My chess opponent was in his mid-20's, appearing to be still of draft age.

My eyes got wide. "You mean that you get a draft deferment for being in the merchant marine?" I castled, to get my King out of the way of the other guy's offensive with his Queen.

"That's right. I'm not going to get my nuts shot off like those fools in the Army, and I get paid a whole lot more than squid (Navy sailors)."

"How do I get seaman's papers?"

"You need a letter of commitment—a statement from a steamship company that they'll give you a job once the Coast Guard gives you your papers. Or you can get one from a union. I'm in the SIU—Seafarers International Union."

"How would I get that kind of letter from the SIU?"

"Well," he said, slowly backing off from his attack on the chess board, "you've got to know somebody who's big in the Union or you have to give a lot of money to piece off the union patrolman who makes the job calls. There's also a school at the hiring hall on Jackson Avenue, for trainees to get put on their first ship."

The game ended in a stalemate and we went our separate ways. I thought about what the seaman had told me. Going to sea seemed a lot more interesting than working on an assembly line. And then there was the Viet Nam factor. I was classified as I-A on two draft cards, in both my real and phony names. On the other hand, getting fingerprinted meant that I would blow my cover because I'd have to do it in my real name. I decided to sit pat until I learned what the Maine detective was going to do.

There was no racism in New Orleans that I saw, as long as everyone knew their place. I started dating a black girl. I can't remember her name—I think it was Angel or Angela. I do remember that she was 18 and angelically beautiful. Our relationship didn't last very long and never got past a goodnight kiss. She lived near Rampart, just past the edge of the French Quarter, and took me home once to meet her parents. They were gracious, treating me politely even though they knew that their daughter and I didn't stand a chance of having a lasting courtship. And her parents were right. Walking to my apartment with her that evening on Dauphine Street, two elderly white women approached us on the sidewalk. One of them spit at me, hitting my shirt just under the collar. I was mortified with embarrassment and never again called upon my would-be girlfriend. So much for that romance.

In addition to being lonely in New Orleans, I desperately wanted to find something to believe in. My upbringing in organized Christianity led me to conclude that it was basically a fraud, run by hypocrites and charlatans. I hoped that black gospel churches in the French Quarter would somehow be different. The congregation at the one I went to welcomed me with open arms. It was on Burgundy Street, in a small, ramshackle wooden building, with about 30 parishioners present the night I walked in and sat in the back pew, hoping not to be noticed. I liked the singing but my New England sensitivities were a little put off by the talking in tongues and by all the laying on of hands to help me see Jesus after I was summoned to the pulpit and told to kneel. I only went there once.

Next I tried a storefront church on Bienville Street that promised understanding of the universe by drinking carrot juice and eating psychedelic mushrooms. That seemed pretty weird, even in 1969, and I was too cheap to buy any mushrooms. I tried the required vegetarian diet for a week. I probably didn't do it right because I had no energy and dragged ass at the factory. After a few visits, I didn't go back to that church either.

I'd earlier read L. Ron Hubbard's book, Dianetics, and was intrigued by some of his theories. Specifically, that one could become "clear"—have no emotional hang-ups—by delving into the past to expose and eliminate en-grams, early traumas that were said to be the source of all psychological problems. Scientology, which followed the teachings of Hubbard, had a church west of Canal in the business district. I think it was on Magazine Street. I called and made an appointment for late one afternoon after I got off first shift.

"Come in." An attractive woman in her late 20s led me into the second floor church, which looked more like an office. She was very friendly and I felt right at home while she asked me about my expectations of Scientology and what Scientology could do for me. Before scheduling my first session on the E-meter—the devise used to detect en-grams—I was given a form to fill out for background information.

"$2.48 an hour! What does that mean?" The woman was reading from the form I'd handed back, in the space marked for income.

"That's my income. I work in a factory."

"You work in a factory!" I nodded. There was a long silence. "I'll call you to schedule your session." Then I got the bum's rush out of the church. She never contacted me.

After that, I realized it was likely that no one had the answer to life's mysteries. I already knew that the promise of an afterlife was bullshit, a sucker-ploy to make people believe they could re-do what they'd fucked up in this life if they gave money to the flim-flam artists who promised everlasting life. The people in the gospel church seemed to be having a good time, but I guessed that they too were expected to put more money than they could afford into the collection plate. Maybe the Existentialists had it right. Maybe there was no forgiveness. Maybe I had to take responsibility in this life for what I did in this life...? I didn't know. The only thing I learned was that seekers of the truth like me were all being taken advantage of by somebody.

Mardi Gras in 1970 might have been the first time New Orleans experienced a large influx of long-hairs (hippies). Fat Tuesday, the day before Lent started on Ash Wednesday, was on February 10th that year. Celebration and parades started ten days earlier. The French Quarter was always littered with drunks, even without the license for excess granted by the carnival. Added to the dereliction were long-hairs living on the street who had either run out of money, taken bad drugs, or been sucked into the culture of alcohol abuse—alcohol comprising the pond upon which the French Quarter seemed to float. I was amazed by the parades during Mardi Gras, but there was also some bad craziness brought on by it. One afternoon I was walking home on Ursulines Street with a full bag of groceries before it was time to go to work on second shift. Three long-hairs were sitting on the corner as I crossed

Bourbon Street. "Hey man," one of them said with an East Coast inflection to his voice, "how do we get to Iberville Street?"

"Go that way," I pointed down Bourbon. "It's about ten blocks." I figured the guy had chosen me to ask directions to an easily-found destination because I hadn't gotten a haircut since I left Seattle. Even though it was far above my shoulders, my hair was still long enough to suggest that I was not a supporter of Richard Nixon.

"I want you to show us the way." The guy came closer. He was my height, a bit wider and maybe five years older than me. I looked into his eyes. They were wild, like a kaleidoscope!

"Bad acid," I thought, but I said out loud: "I've got to get home with these groceries. Just go that way," I gestured, "and you'll come to Iberville." I turned away and started walking along Ursulines. It was chilly that day and I wore a beige sweater.

"I said I want you to take us there!" The guy grabbed the back of my sweater. I kept walking and the back of the sweater ripped off in his hand. I put my grocery sack on the sidewalk and turned around. It was time to fight!

I didn't really want to fight because the guy had two buddies, plus it would make me late for work. I didn't have to because the two friends ran up to restrain my assailant. I walked home to put my groceries away. I figured that spring was coming and I wouldn't need a sweater anymore in New Orleans.

The cops were out of control during Carnival that year. I already knew that the New Orleans Police Department was brutal and corrupt. From behind my chili dog cart I'd watch them do whatever they wanted —or rather, whatever they thought they could get away with. During Mardi Gras, the cops decided that it was open season on hippies. One night I sat on a second story balcony watching a parade on Royal Street with two long-hairs I'd met from the University of Maine. They were on a road trip to see the USA and I let them stay in my apartment for a few nights. A horse-mounted police officer approached, riding alongside one of the floats. When the cop spotted us he pulled a Billy club out of its loop on his gun belt and whacked me on the knee. That hurt! He trotted off without explanation.

Mardi Gras was exciting, but I was glad when it was over.

Not long after Mardi Gras, the Meat Cutters Union announced an election for president of the local at the Wesson Oil plant to be held early that spring. I was still resentful about being forced to join the union and, for a lark, declared my candidacy. That was possibly the stupidest thing I'd ever done. The local was better than 95% black and I was a white boy with a snowball's chance in hell of winning an election. The young guys stopped inviting me out on Fridays, and the older guys at the Wesson plant stopped shooting the shit with me during breaks. I began to get a bit nervous about accidents at work.

The merchant marine started looking more attractive. I decided that the Maine detective was bluffing about coming to get me, even if he could find out where I was. "Anyway," I thought, "he won't be able to find me, even under my real name, because I'll be on different ships all over the world." The hiring hall for the Seafarers International Union was at 630 Jackson Avenue, along the bus route to the factory, only a few blocks from the ferry across the Mississippi. I started getting off the bus a few stops early on those afternoons I worked second shift.

The SIU union hall was an impressive two-story structure of white stucco with decorative black cast iron on the outside. It stood out from the run-down buildings on Jackson Avenue. Inside was an open, auditorium-like space with a counter for job calls in front of the west wall. Behind the counter was a large bulletin board with a listing of ships in port down the left side and a row of job ratings along the top. Numbers—mostly 1 but sometimes 2 and occasionally even 3—were inserted in a grid, showing the numbers of each position available on each ship. There was a heavy-set Italian-looking guy in front of the job-board smoking a cigar. "I want to get into the school here," I said, thinking that he must be the SIU Patrolman who called out jobs. "How do I do it?"

"Go talk to Don Collins." He jerked his thumb toward a door to one side of the job board.

"Thanks." I walked up to the door and knocked.

"Yeah?" a loud, hoarse voice answered after a short silence. I walked into the small office. Don Collins was clean-shaven with slicked-back hair—slim and of average height and build like me, but about 40 and dressed as though he was on his way to bet the horses at a racetrack. There was a heavy scent of cologne in the air and an ashtray overflowing with cigarette butts. "What do you want?" He had his feet up on the desk.

"I want to get into the school here."

"Why should I let you?" I thought I smelled a trace of alcohol when he spoke.

"Because I'm a hard worker and will make a good seaman."

"There're a lot of young punks who want to get into this school. Leave your name at the counter. I'll let you know if there's an opening."

"Do you know when an opening is expected?" I persisted.

"No," he said brusquely as he stood up. "I've got an appointment." He shooed me out of his office.

I gave my name and address to the guy in front of the job board and left the SIU Hall to catch the ferry to Gretna.

I was back the next day. Don Collins ran me out of his office again, but I was back a day later. And the day after that. I kept pestering him, leaving him notes late in the afternoon on those days when I was on first shift and he wasn't there. I can't remember how long it took but he finally got tired of me bugging him. "OK, you can start on Monday. Bring a suitcase because you'll be living in back of the Hall until I put you on a ship."

I quit my job, gave notice to my landlord, and went back to using my real name. On March 16, 1970 my head was shaved, I put on a white uniform—like those worn by orderlies in a hospital—and became a student at the Harry Lundeberg School of Seamanship.

Harry Lundeberg was the first president of the SIU, when it formed in 1938 following a split with the Congress of Industrial Organizations (CIO). A rival union, the NMU (National Maritime Union), was more left-leaning and allowed black seamen to join. Under the umbrella of the CIO, the NMU was accused of being a Communist front organization, while the SIU remained in the more conservative American Federation of Labor (AFL). The AFL and CIO would later enter into an uneasy alliance-of-necessity, merging in 1955.

I didn't know any of this history when I was handed a mop on March 16th. There were a few black seamen in the SIU Hall but the only jobs they bid for during job calls were in the Steward Department, as cooks or messmen. I also didn't know that the union at the time was in legal battles with government agencies over integration of the deck and engine departments aboard SIU ships.

What I did know was that I was made to sign a chit for $2.50 to get my head shaved—to be later deducted from my wages after I caught a ship—when at the time one could get a good professional haircut for half that price. Along with the other trainees I was also given a carton of cigarettes every week and required to sign chits for roughly double the going price in a store. For spending money we were given $7/week, but were required to sign a chit for $10 each time it was handed out.

There were maybe a dozen of us at the school when I started. We were housed in a small, two-story white frame dormitory in back of the union hall. Our tenure there was until a ship in the harbor couldn't fill a billet from the regular job calls and an extra seaman was needed. I was there for 44 days.

We slept in bunks, several to a room, and ate in the hiring hall's cafeteria, located at the far right corner on the first floor. As trainees, we were given grunt jobs around the union hall. It was basically a free labor academy, even though I suspect the SIU was getting funding from ship owners or the government to run a school. The whole time I was there I was never so much as shown a lifejacket.

We got up at 0600 for breakfast and the day's labor. Sometimes we worked as waiters during political events hosted upstairs at the union hall. The second story of the hall was a large open space with a stage and podium for speakers at one end. The political shindigs would go on until after midnight and sometimes as late as 0200. We'd have to clean up after that and still be expected to turn to at 0600 the next morning. Some of the trainees couldn't get up after maybe three hours of sleep. Once I watched Don Collins drag a trainee from his bunk onto the floor while hurling obscenities and kicking him in the head for not getting up on time. Don Collins was a bully and a drunk. Rumor had it that he and some of the other union officials were on pills as well. I figured I could whip Don Collins if he ever tried to kick me in the head, but that would be the end of my prospects in the merchant marine.

My fellow trainees were an odd lot, mostly local boys from Louisiana. There wasn't much camaraderie at the so-called school; it was more just a struggle to survive. The turnover rate was high. Maybe half of those who were in the program when I started lasted long enough to be put on a ship. At the time, judges in coastal states typically gave a choice to rowdy young males caught breaking the law: 'Go to jail, join the Army, or go to sea.' In Louisiana at least, those minor criminals who knew someone in the SIU ended up with me in the building behind the New Orleans hiring hall. Only one was a black kid. He was tough—he had to be to survive in that dormitory. One of the few trainees I became friends with was from Arkansas, Ricky Bosnick. He told me that both his father and his 18-year-old brother were on death row. The worst of those in the program was a swamp-boy from the bayous named Boudreaux. He was about 6-foot tall, wide and muscular. He had a bad complexion and was butt-ugly. Most of all though, Boudreaux was just flat-out mean. He beat the shit out of two trainees and acted like there would be others. I figured that it was only a matter of time before it was my turn. I decided that I needed to get Boudreaux before he got me.

Seven dollars a week didn't go very far, even in 1970 New Orleans. I knew about a bar, not too far from the SIU Hall, that had nickel beer night on Wednesdays. Twelve ounce glasses of beer were sold for 5 cents each. A few of my fellow trainees knew about nickel beer night but this intelligence was not shared with Boudreaux. Boudreaux did anything he could think of to get drunk or stoned, including sniffing aerosol from spray cans and smoking scrapings from banana peels, or parsley that he'd been told was marijuana. He also had a hypodermic needle that he used to shoot himself up with various liquids, practicing for when he could afford heroin. He was an animal! I'd read somewhere about a junkie looking for a cheap high, who died after he shot himself up with cold wine. The temperature difference was said to have caused a blood clot and killed him. I thought that might be the way to get rid of Boudreaux for good.

"Hey, Boudreaux," I said to him one Wednesday evening after we were let go by Don Collins. There were no political functions that night and we got off early. "Want to get high?" I'd put the dregs of a bottle of white port—fortified wine with an alcohol content of 20%—into the freezer of the little refrigerator that was on the second floor of our dormitory. Boudreaux was very interested and came over to where I was sitting on a bunk. "If you shoot up this wine, you'll get really drunk, really fast. I'm going to give you the rest of this bottle." I handed him the white port, which had about two ounces left at the bottom.

He grunted in appreciation and ran off to get his hypodermic needle. After I saw that Boudreaux was really going to shoot up ice-cold white port, I left to make sure that I had an alibi when he did.

I went to nickel beer night with a couple of the trainees. We had a good time but didn't stay late because we'd be rousted at 0600. I didn't say a word about fortified wine and a hypodermic needle. When I got back to the SIU dormitory, there were no ambulances or police cars so I figured they'd already left. I went inside to see what had happened. Boudreaux was not only still alive, he was running around and acting happy!

"Didn't you shoot up the white port?" I whispered. He said he did and that it got him really drunk. He thanked me profusely. After that, Boudreaux acted like I was his best friend.

The union hall was in a black neighborhood of New Orleans—still called a Negro area back then. SIU seamen were all white, with the exception of some in the Steward Department. The two cooks in the union cafeteria were black. I managed to get myself put into a steady job there as Sandwich and Salad Man about halfway through my training at the Harry Lundeberg School of Seamanship. I knew Don Collins, the Director of the school, was afraid to antagonize the two cooks, so that gave me a measure of protection. The cafeteria closed shortly after the last job call at 1600 (4 p.m.).

The most popular sandwiches at the cafeteria were oyster po' boys. So many were ordered that the small Gulf oysters I used to make po' boys were delivered in one-gallon cans. One afternoon I stole a gallon of oysters from the cafeteria refrigerator. After it got dark I took the oysters close to the river, where there was a black bar just off Jackson on a side street. The bar served food and had a kitchen in back. I went into the bar and approached a woman who looked like she was in charge, telling her I'd trade the oysters for free drinks that evening. I pulled out a jackknife and pried the lid off the gallon-can. When the woman looked inside the can and saw how many oysters I'd brought, her eyes got wide and she pushed me toward the kitchen. After I handed the gallon can to the man cooking in the kitchen, I thought he was going to hug me when he took a look. There were enough oysters for everyone in the bar that evening and I became a honky messiah of sorts. I drank free beer and danced my ass off with lots of different

17

women. A good time was had by all! Even though I was half drunk, there was a spring in my step as I went back to the dormitory around midnight.

It wasn't always fun and games being white in a black neighborhood. One night I left the union hall for a destination I no longer recall. A few blocks away, two black guys about my age approached me and aggressively asked for a cigarette. "I don't have one," I lied. I didn't like their attitude. If they'd asked nicely I would have given each of them a Lucky Strike from the pack in my breast pocket. There was a bit of glaring at each other and then I walked away. I'd gone about 10 yards when one of them threw a soda bottle. He had a good aim because the bottle hit me just above the back of my neck and then shattered on the street. It didn't hurt so much as surprise me, and I whirled around to fight. The two black guys were in the same place where I'd left them, and weren't pursuing me. Instead they said something about whitey being on their turf and slowly walked away.

Job calls were at the top of the hour during weekdays and on Saturday mornings. It was the height of the Viet Nam war and lots of ships were moving in and out of port. Dozens of seamen gathered in front of the job board, shoving and jostling each other during the job calls. There was A, B and C seniority, determining the preference of who got the best jobs. A C-card was anyone without an A-book or B-book who had no union seniority and might just as well have walked in off the street looking for a job. Trainees like me were shipped out after no B-book wanted the job on a particular ship, before it was given to a C-card. Shipping was brisk during April 1970 and trainees were getting shipped out fairly rapidly. I figured it would be my turn before the end of the month.

Sometime during the middle of April the current crop of trainees were taken to the Coast Guard to get issued seamen's papers. We were given a physical exam, fingerprinted and photographed. A requirement left over from the two world wars, 20/20 vision was required for the merchant marine—even though the steamship companies, along with the Army, would take anybody they could get for Viet Nam. I was near-sighted and wore contact lenses, but passed the vision test because no one asked about contact lenses.

Don Collins didn't always put trainees on ships in order of seniority. Those who sucked up to him, or had union connections, left earlier. Those he didn't like left a little later. Even though I hated Don Collins, I'd managed to avoid his wrath. Near the end of April, it was my turn and I figured that my ship would come in any day.

On April 23, 1970 President Nixon eliminated any future draft deferments based upon employment—including those for merchant seamen—by executive order. He also wanted to eliminate deferments for students, who were a constant pain in his side, but he couldn't do it by executive order and Congress wouldn't go along with him on that. That sort of pulled the rug out from under my feet. A deferment was the main reason I'd wanted to join the merchant marine. The change for deferments wasn't retroactive but, technically, I wasn't a merchant seaman until I got my first job—I'd missed out by a few days, at most. If I'd sucked up to Don Collins and shipped out earlier I wouldn't have had to worry about the draft. "Should I go through with this?" I wondered.

I weighed my options. The draft had gone to a lottery in 1969 for everybody older than me. There were 366 numbers drawn, one for each day of the year, and assigned by one's birthday. Numbers for my birth year, 1951, would be drawn on July 1, 1970. According to an article I read in the New Orleans Times-Picayune, the Army expected to draft less than half the numbers to be drawn in the 1970 lottery. I figured I was born lucky and wasn't too worried about drawing a number low enough to be drafted. I'd quit my job at the factory and given up my apartment. I didn't have much to go back to if I dropped out of the SIU school. Even if I did, and got another job on land, I'd still be at risk of getting drafted. The alternative was getting a student deferment. I didn't really want to go to college. My grades in high school weren't that hot and getting into college was not a sure thing even though I had high scores on the Scholastic Aptitude Test. And even if I got into college, there was the problem of staying in—to keep my deferment. I still had some money in a savings account at the Whitney National Bank, but it wouldn't last forever. After a semester, or two at the most, I'd be right back where I started, with no deferment—and this time with no savings. And then there was the detective in Maine. I was pretty sure he was running a bluff about coming to get me, but I wasn't 100% sure. I'd now been fingerprinted. If he wasn't bluffing, I'd prefer to be on a ship so there was some ocean separating us. I decided to stay at the SIU hall until I got shipped out. To hedge my bet about getting a high lottery number, I wrote to my aunt and uncle and asked them to send me an application to the University of Washington.

I shipped out a few days later. On April 28th I was given the job of Crew Messman on the S.S. Del Valle, owned by the Delta Steamship Co. and bound for Viet Nam. I was told to report for duty that morning. I'm told that I was the first trainee to be handed a B-book from the New Orleans hiring hall—certainly the first one who didn't have to pay for it. That was important if I wanted to stay in the merchant marine. B-books had a lot better chance of getting jobs than did C-cards. I took a taxi to the Army Docks in New Orleans.

Sister ship to the S.S. Del Valle
(I couldn't find a photo of my ship)

The S.S. Del Valle was a freighter with masts and booms over five cargo holds. Three of the holds were forward of the superstructure—which contained living spaces for the crew—and two behind it. I would later learn that the 8,000-ton Del Valle was 459 feet long and 63 feet wide. Much later, not that I cared, I learned that the ship was propelled by two steam boilers and two turbines putting out 6,000 horsepower. A C-2 class freighter, the Del Valle was built in Wilmington, North Carolina in 1944, one of 173 C-2s that were launched during World War II. I walked up the gangway with my suitcase.

"Crew Messman," I told the seaman at the head of the gangway. "Where's my room?" The man guarding ingress onto the ship was about my size but a little older, with wavy black hair. He was muscular and had an anchor tattooed on his right bicep. I would later learn that he was an Able Seaman (AB) from Mississippi named Jimmie Singleton.

"Your fo'c'sle is starboard side, aft," he gestured. He must have seen that I looked confused. "You're a cherry, aren't you? Follow me." The AB led me to my fo'c'sle, stopping at the doorway. The door was open, secured by a hook on the wall inside. "The Judge has the bottom bunk. He's the BR (bedroom steward)."

"The Judge...?" I looked into a space about 15 feet deep and 10 feet wide with a porthole at the end. A double-bunk was on the wall to my right (aft) with a sink beyond it, just before the open porthole. On the left side, across from the sink, were two lockers and a small desk. On the top bunk a blanket and thin blue bedspread were rolled up at the foot of a bare mattress. A pillow lay at the head of the bed.

"That's what we call him. He used to be a lawyer or a judge, I think in New Orleans. He's older than hell. I don't know why he's going to sea. He'll get you your linen when he finishes making bunks for the officers topside."

"I should probably go help with breakfast," I said, throwing my suitcase onto the top bunk.

"Don't worry about it. Get settled in first. The Steward is fat and lazy, a sorry son-of-bitch from Mobile who's afraid of his own shadow. Anyway, breakfast is almost over and your Pantryman is getting OT for covering the messhall."

"Thanks," I said as the AB went back to the gangway. I took his advice and put my gear into the locker that was unlocked and empty. The Judge's locker had a small combination lock hanging from the latch. After that I walked around to check out my new home. Toilets and showers were just forward of my fo'c'sle. Most of the crew quarters were on the main deck, wrapped around a huge space in the middle for the engine room. Officers slept on the upper decks. The radio room, bridge, and Captain's cabin were higher still. Below the main deck were various storerooms, some refrigerated, for food and supplies.

The Judge was in our fo'c'sle when I returned. He was slender and stooped, hair totally white, and had to be well into his 70s. I learned later that there was no mandatory retirement age for merchant seamen, although most didn't live nearly as long as the Judge. "I'm John, the new Crew Messman." I stuck out my hand.

"John Butler." He tentatively shook my hand. "I brought your linen," he said, motioning toward my bunk. I saw two sheets and a pillowcase under two bath towels, two face towels, two bars of Dial soap and one of Lava, and a packet with 12 boxes of wooden matches. There was also a folded white linen jacket, which I guessed was for me to put on when waiting tables. The Judge didn't say anything after that. He wasn't much for conversation. Over the next three months the only information I got out of him about his past was that he got bored with retirement and went to sea for something to do.

I figured that I'd better go check out the messhall before lunch. It was in the forward part of the house (superstructure) on the main deck, just behind the galley on the starboard side. Four tables, each with four chairs sitting atop steel tubes bolted to the deck, were in a space about 25-foot square with a low ceiling and cement deck painted red. Short red-checkered curtains hung over three portholes. A forward door connected to the pantry—a small, rectangular space with a large dishwashing machine on a stainless steel countertop. To the right, in the pantry facing forward was another identical pantry for the saloon where the officers ate. The saloon itself, forward of the saloon pantry was slightly larger than the messhall with fewer chairs around a single, long table. A door to the left in the crew pantry went into the large galley. I walked in and saw two black cooks between a long stainless steel counter and two giant, side-by-side stoves. The larger of the two whirled around when I walked into the galley. "Who are you?" He was about 6'2", broad-shouldered, and held a French knife in his hand. His eyes were angry and looked like lasers.

"Crew Messman. Name's John." I was so scared that I forgot to use my Southern accent.

"I'm the Chief Cook." He appeared to relax a bit. "Call me J.C."

The other cook took off his apron and walked out from behind the counter. "I'm Harry, the Third Cook," he said, extending his hand. Harry was tall and slender, with a wisp of mustache and goatee. When I shook hands I noticed that he had long, delicate fingers.

"When am I supposed to start working lunch?" I asked Harry. "This is my first ship."

"1030. Lunch is served from 1130 to 1230. After you clean up, you're off from 1300 to 1600 before you set up for dinner. You serve the evening meal from 1700 to 1800 and then knock off at 1830."

"What time do I have to get up tomorrow morning?"

"An Ordinary or one of the ABs will call you at 0600. You turn to at 0630 to get ready for breakfast—served from 0730 to 0830. You clean the messhall and knock off at 0930."

"Thanks, Harry." I looked at the clock in the galley. "It's almost 1030. I'd best start setting up." I went back to my fo'c'sle for the linen jacket and then returned to the messhall.

"Are you the first-tripper?" I was looking into the little messhall refrigerator after I put condiments and silverware on my tables for lunch—all four covered with red-checkered tablecloths that matched the curtains. I looked up and saw a stocky white boy with a thin mustache standing in front of me. He was slightly shorter than me and about 25 years old.

"Yeah. Name's John." I stuck out my hand.

"Paul. You've got to make the cold drinks—iced-tea, Kool-aid, and ice water," he said as we shook hands. I later learned that Paul was from Ohio and had recently gotten out of the Navy.

I finished setting up the tables, made the cold drinks and then went into the galley to fetch the menus. Paul was making individual salads. As Crew Pantryman, he was also responsible for preparing the desserts and doing the dishes.

"Impressive menu," I thought, "even though some words are misspelled." For lunch, three entrees and three vegetables were listed, along with soup, three "hore d'oeuvres," and two desserts. The dinner choices were just as impressive. I noticed that the vegetable selections

23

for both meals were decidedly Southern, including turnip greens, mustard greens, okra, butter beans, and black-eyed peas. Grits figured prominently on the breakfast menu. I put copies of the menu on each table and was ready to go, 10 minutes ahead of time, at 1120 hours. That was a good thing because some of the crew started filtering in 10 minutes early. I learned that members of the deck and engine departments who were on the 12-4 watch (am and pm) came in early so they could eat, have time for a a smoke, and then relieve the 8-12 watch shortly before noon.

I took orders from the early arrivals and then went to the galley to see if J.C. and Harry would serve them yet. They did. It turned out that all the meals started early and usually ended early, as a matter of shipboard courtesy, so the steward department could finish up and knock off early. By the same token, the watchstanders typically relieved each other 15 minutes early. That meant that the 8-12 watch, in both deck and engine departments, came in to eat lunch before noon and left well before lunch technically ended at 1230.

I didn't have to work too hard and was basically a waiter in a small restaurant. There were 12 officers who ate in the saloon, served by the Saloon Messman and Saloon Pantryman, and 30 unlicensed seamen who ate in my messhall. Of those, I didn't have to wait on the nine of us in the steward department. Many in the 4-8 watch were ashore or asleep and didn't get up for lunch. I never had to re-set any of my 16 place settings during the first meal I served. My job was a piece of cake!

I was breaking down my tables at 1220 hours and bringing the dishes to Paul, when the Chief Steward walked in. "Are you the Messman?" He looked to be in his 50s but was probably a lot younger. The Steward was white, had a big belly and precious few teeth left in his gums. I learned that his name was Louis Cayten, from Mobile, Alabama where he used to drive a taxicab. I smelled booze on his breath and guessed he had just come back from ashore.

"Right. Name's John." I stuck out my hand.

"I want this messhall spic'n'span after every meal, Messman," he said after we shook. His hand felt clammy. "The Old Man's a stickler about cleanliness. You need to sweep and mop carefully three times a day."

"Yes, sir," I responded. The Steward grabbed one of the menus and left by way of the after door in the messhall, rather than going through the galley where Harry and J.C. were wrapping up.

I dutifully swept and mopped the messhall, and then went back to my fo'c'sle to lie down and let all these new developments sink in, eventually dozing off.

At 1600 I jumped off the top bunk and went back to the messhall to prepare for dinner. Dinner went much like lunch did. The exception was that there were new faces at the tables. The 4-8 watch ate in shifts. In the deck department, two ABs and the Ordinary Seaman ate one at a time so that they could relieve each other. In the engine department, the Oiler came up first to eat, and then went back into the engine room so the Fireman could come up. Some in the 8-12 and 12-4 watches didn't show for dinner and were probably ashore. From the scuttlebutt I overheard while serving the crew who did show, it seemed that a lot of them would be getting off in the next port, Mobile, so they wouldn't have to sign on for a voyage to Viet Nam.

I tidied up the messhall after dinner, and had it swept and mopped well before 1830 hours. I had the evening to kill and no desire to go ashore. There was a recreation room on the port side of the main deck just aft of the galley. No one was there and it was dark. I turned on the light and saw a large, round table in one corner, a black-and-white television on a platform just beneath the ceiling and a large bookshelf filled with paperbacks. I walked over to check out the selection. The paperback books were almost all murder mysteries and detective thrillers. A thick red book with a black swastika on the cover caught my eye, *The Rise and Fall of the Third Reich* by William Shirer. I grabbed it and went back to my fo'c'sle.

There was a small tubular light on the wall next to my pillow. After taking a shower, further arranging my belongings and writing a letter to my aunt and uncle, I read Shirer's book until I fell asleep.

"Time to turn to, Messman." I didn't see who woke me up because he left the fo'c'sle as soon as he saw that I was awake. It was 0600 and morning light streamed through the porthole. The Judge got out of his bunk quickly, while I rubbed my eyes and wondered where I was.

Back in the messhall, I started setting up for breakfast. The large can of ground coffee was empty and I couldn't make a fresh batch. The

Pantryman was messing around with grapefruit halves. "Hey, Paul, where's the coffee stashed?"

"Go below," he said. "It's in the for'd storeroom on the port side."

I went down a steep, narrow staircase to the storerooms, forward of the engine room. The storeroom my Pantryman described was lined with metal shelves that were stacked to the ceiling with canned fruits and vegetables. There was a section with a pile of green three-pound cans of ground coffee. I don't remember the brand name on the cans—it was one I'd never heard of—but I do remember that the fine print stated that the brand was a subsidiary of Coca-Cola. I went back up and brewed two pots of coffee from the can I brought up from the storeroom.

"This tastes like shit!" I complained to the Pantryman after I poured a cup of my own coffee. I'd been spoiled by good coffee in New Orleans, with chicory, like that served in the French Market.

"So what?" Paul said. "All coffee is supposed to do is wake you up and make you take a crap." My first customer, an AB on the 8-12 watch, came in and waited to be served.

J.C., the Chief Cook, was not in the galley when I put in the first order. The Third Cook, Harry, was standing next to a white guy who was playing with an omelet on one of the stove tops. I learned that he was the Second Cook and Baker. He got up in the wee hours to bake and help the Third Cook with breakfast while the Chief Cook slept. The Chief Cook in turn worked through the afternoon while the Second Cook was off for the rest of the day. The Third Cook got three hours off between lunch and dinner, 1300-1600, like I did. The only thing I remember about the Second Cook and Baker is that he had a black-and-gray moustache, wore glasses, and was from Puerto Rico. I guessed that he was in his mid-50s.

Breakfast went without incident. I overheard the deck gang talking about the Del Valle leaving that afternoon. After cleaning up the messhall, I walked out on deck to check on the cargo operation. I had a smoke and watched as the booms lifted pallets stacked with crates up from the dock. There were also some large rolls of barbed wire being lifted aboard. The pallets were lowered into the forward holds. I didn't get close enough to read the markings on the crates but assumed that the contents were for the war effort in Viet Nam where our cargo was destined.

The S.S. Del Valle cast off from the Army Docks after I worked lunch and left New Orleans bound for Mobile, Alabama.

Harry, the Third Cook, had written down my pay scale on the back of a menu. As Crew Messman, I was to be paid a base wage of $364.58 a month. Weekends, holidays and any work over eight hours per day were paid at an overtime rate of $2.73/hour. After lunch was over I went to the fantail at the back of the ship for a cigarette as we steamed down the Mississippi toward the Gulf of Mexico. I did some mental arithmetic while watching flat Louisiana tidelands that were riddled with small waterways. I'd be making almost $600/month before taxes even if the steward didn't let me work overtime in the afternoons. That was far more than I made at the Wesson Oil factory, and I wouldn't have to pay for rent and food!

Dinner went smoothly. That evening I wrote a letter, read for a bit and went to sleep with dreams of riches floating through my head.

After breakfast the next morning, I cleaned the messhall and then went out on deck, on the starboard side just forward of the house, to look at the Gulf of Mexico. The Third Cook was already there, smoking a cigarette. I pulled out a Lucky and stood next to him at the rail. "When will we get to Mobile, Harry?"

"Today. I'm not sure when—maybe during lunch."

"How fast does this ship go," I asked.

"Fifteen knots, maybe 15-and-a-half. That's less than 20 miles per hour."

"Hey, thanks for writing down what I get for wages. This is the most money I've ever made!"

"You'll make more," Harry said, "when we get to Viet Nam. We get a 100% pay bonus on base wages while we're in the war zone."

"That's even better!" I said. "Who's paying that?"

"The government," he said. "Most guys don't want to be on this run. You'll see a mess of them pile off before we sign foreign articles, and then we'll get a load of motherfuckers from Mobile on here."

"Are you staying on?"

"J.C. is making the trip and I will too — I just keep my head down and do my job. J.C. don't take no shit from crackers, and the Steward— he leaves our galley alone." Harry squinted toward the horizon. I followed his gaze and saw a column of water shooting up into clouds—a meeting of sea and sky. The column seemed to be moving towards us.

"What's that?!"

"A waterspout," Harry replied matter-of-factly.

"What will happen if it gets close?"

"It will pick this ship up and spin it in the air." The waterspout was moving fast over the water, seemingly aimed right at us.

"Aren't you worried about that?" I asked nervously.

"John," Harry said calmly, 'that waterspout is five miles off. How much chance we got of getting hit? I'm going back to the galley." I remained at the rail, transfixed, as the waterspout seemingly got ever closer. It literally sucked thousands—if not millions —of gallons of water into the clouds. In the face of such incredible force it was futile to go to one of the lifeboats or even get my lifejacket. I watched in dread, my heart pounding, until the waterspout passed behind us.

Looking back, after my panic had subsided, I realized that the waterspout never got within two or three miles of the ship.

We tied up in Mobile, Alabama on April 30th. I can't remember much about Mobile and don't know if I went ashore. I do remember that a few old biddies came aboard from some sort of church society for seamen. They brought lots of books and stocked the shelves in the recreation room. The books were mostly pulp fiction and religious treatises but I spotted some novels by Russian authors like Chekhov and Dostoevsky that I snatched up and took to my fo'c'sle.

The next afternoon a Shipping Commissioner came aboard to preside over the signing of foreign articles. Foreign articles, I would soon learn, meant that one was bound to the ship—on pain of imprisonment for desertion—until the ship returned to the United States. Shipping Commissioners were a hangover from earlier times—needed primarily for long voyages during the days of sail when shipping companies were known to do anything it took to get a crew for long voyages. Their tactics included using crimps and liquor, women, trickery, or a shanghai—as trips to that city in China were called by seamen who signed on for the voyage while unconscious. Shipping Commissioners were supposed to ensure that seamen who signed foreign articles were doing so voluntarily. With strong unions, better wages and shorter voyages, the job of Shipping Commissioner was largely superfluous and would soon be eliminated by Congress.

The Commissioner who came aboard the Del Valle was about my size but 30 years older, with a thin mustache, balding head, and the mousey mannerisms of a bureaucrat. I signed foreign articles in front of the Commissioner but maybe a third of the crew did not. They left the ship and were replaced by seamen dispatched from the SIU hiring hall in Mobile.

More military cargo was loaded in Mobile, the loading continuing into the night. The cargo being loaded—one of the longshoremen told me—included some sort of liquid asphalt for use in Viet Nam. The longshoreman who told me that was a black guy I'd got to talking to in the recreation room after dinner that Friday evening while he was on a break and I walked in to listen to the evening news on TV. He took out a bag of snus and snorted a pinch. "Want some?" he asked.

"What is it?"

"Some calls it snoos and others call it snuff. All I know is that it does me right. Here." He handed me the bag. I copied what I'd seen him do, taking a small amount of what looked like powdered tobacco between my thumb and forefinger and then inhaling it up my right nostril. I started sneezing and coughing, my eyes watering. "You'll get used to it," said the longshoreman.

"Damn!" I doubted I'd ever get used to snus and didn't think I wanted to. The longshoreman rambled on about snus and about how much cargo he pilfered off the docks while it was being loaded. In the background, I heard a TV newsman say that President Nixon announced that he'd escalated the war by sending U.S. troops into Cambodia.

The S.S. Del Valle left the next afternoon, bound for Port Arthur, Texas. It was early May. We were in Port Arthur for a couple of days, topping off our cargo with trucks and tanks. They were piled so high above the forward holds that the deck department had to build a walkway of wooden planks on top of the vehicles for access to the bow from the house. The vehicles had logos stenciled on the side in white paint with the large letters ARVN (Army of the Republic of Viet Nam).

Port Arthur was a rough-and-tumble town of oil refineries on Sabine Lake, right on the Louisiana state line. In addition to the Sabine

River, Sabine Lake was also fed by the Neches River, part of which constitutes the border between Texas and Louisiana. I got a $40 draw against my wages and went ashore at least once. I don't remember much about the town but I do remember having a beer in an all-white bar, even though the population of Port Arthur seemed to be half black. When the guy on the next barstool learned that I was from out of town, he asked: "What's the difference between a coon-ass and a jackass?"

"I give up," I gamely responded.

"The Neches River!" With that he exploded into laughter. "Bring this boy a beer, on me," he yelled at the bartender, rewarding himself and me for a joke he thought well told.

Back on the ship, that first day in Port Arthur, I finished cleaning up early after dinner and went into the recreation room to watch the 6:00 news on TV. My Pantryman, Paul, was right behind me. The rec room was filled with longshoremen on break—most of whom were black. Walter Cronkite announced that students had rioted all over the country after President Nixon announced that he'd sent troops into Cambodia. "The Ohio National Guard was called out to quell rioting at Kent State University. The Guardsmen opened fire on the rioting students," Cronkite somberly reported, "and four were killed." The longshoremen started cheering! I thought I heard my Pantryman cheering, too.

"Why are you happy about them getting shot?" I whispered to Paul. "I thought you were from Ohio."

"I am, but those hippies deserved it!"

My Pantryman's response surprised me. Even though he had short hair, I'd seen him smoking pot on the fantail with some of the other young guys in the crew. I just assumed that smoking marijuana meant that he was against the war, Nixon and everything else that seemed to separate the younger generation (at least up North) from the World War II generation who was running the country. "A lot of them weren't longhairs," I pointed out.

"So what? They seem to have a lot of free time to demonstrate instead of studying. They need to get a job!" The news was almost over. I decided to go to my fo'c'sle and read.

We were in Port Arthur until May 6th, taking on cargo. Foreign Articles were still open, which meant some in the crew could get off the ship without penalty while we were still in the continental United

30

States. Both Electricians, an Oiler and two Ordinary Seamen (OS) all quit. All but one or two of them were replaced by seamen dispatched from the SIU hiring hall in Houston.

The S.S. Del Valle went upriver to Beaumont, Texas where she took on bunker fuel for the oil-fired furnaces. On May 7th, Foreign Articles were closed. The deck department cast off and we headed down the Neches River, back to the Gulf of Mexico, and steamed for the Panama Canal.

It would take four days to reach Panama. The first day we were at sea, far away from the coast, I used my afternoon break to lie in the sun and read, pretending that I was a wealthy passenger on a luxury liner. I took a cot up to the top deck, next to the smokestack, and stretched out with my book. I fell asleep, face down, and woke up just before it was time to turn to for the evening meal. I was beet-red on the back of my legs and my back must have looked the same. "This is the worst sunburn I've ever gotten," I thought, "and I was only out here for three hours. Maybe the sun's more intense away from land, where there's no pollution...?" I worked dinner without a problem but the next morning my legs were swollen huge, like I had elephantiasis or something—so big that I couldn't fit into my blue jeans. I also felt dizzy and almost fell over while wrestling with my pants. I told the Judge that I didn't think I could work breakfast.

"Sun poison," the Steward announced when he followed the Judge into our fo'c'sle later that morning. I later learned that the Judge stood in for me and served breakfast. "Knock off for the rest of the day. The best thing for sun poison is to take a hot shower. That will open your pores and let the heat escape." I spent the rest of the day, feverish, in my bunk. I got up only long enough to take a shower. I didn't know until years later that the Steward was giving me bad advice, but it might have worked. I turned on the shower water as hot as I could without screaming in pain.

Whether it was the hot shower or lying in my rack for a day, the swelling was almost gone by the next morning and I had no further problems.

While setting up for breakfast when I was back at my job, I saw Jimmy Johnson, AB on the 4-8 watch, come in and write on the messhall blackboard, "Poker 2000 hrs Rec Room." Jimmy Johnson was in his mid-30s and hailed from northern Alabama. Tall and clean-shaven with a square jaw, he was what women likely would consider handsome. He was also a card shark.

I looked forward to the game that night. I was good with numbers and had won quite a bit of money in high school playing poker and blackjack with small-time drug dealers and others who gambled their earnings from part-time jobs. I considered myself a hot-shot at cards. I figured that I couldn't get pushed out of the game with high betting because I still had left most of the $40 draw I'd taken in Port Arthur.

After dinner that evening I wrote a letter to one of my sisters and then went to the Recreation Room at 2000 hours. Jimmy Johnson was sitting at the table, along with two others. There were seven chairs at the table. "Are you in, Messman?" Jimmy Johnson asked.

"I'm in." I pulled out $30 and sat down. Next to me was a barrel-chested AB on the 12-4 watch named Ruffner. He was from Houston and looked about 30. Across from Ruffner, on the other side of Jimmy Johnson, sat Benny Brinson the Bo's'n, who hailed from New Orleans. The Bo's'n was fit for his likely 45 years—give-or-take, with a ruddy complexion and hair that was white, not gray. After I sat down, the seat on my left was taken by Phil, the other AB on the 4-8 watch with Jimmy Johnson, who looked slightly younger than the Bo's'n. A few minutes later the last two seats were taken by Paul, my Pantryman, and Louis Broomfield, the Saloon Pantryman. Louis was a black kid with a big nose. He was small, but aggressive enough that no one messed with him. At 16 he was the youngest guy on the ship. (There is no minimum age for joining the merchant marine.)

It was dealer's choice with a 25-cent ante. Betting was pot-limit with no limit on the number of raises. The games of choice were seven- and five-card stud, and five-card draw with jacks-or-better to open. "High card deals." Jimmy Johnson slapped down the deck in the middle of the table. We all drew cards and turned them upright. "Benny's high," Jimmy announced after the Bo's'n turned over a king.

"Seven-card stud," the Bo's'n said as he shuffled the cards. "Ante up." He threw a quarter in the middle of the table and everybody did the same. "Cut," he said, passing the deck to the Saloon Pantryman to his right. The Bo's'n dealt clockwise, starting with Jimmy Johnson on his left. Everybody got two cards, face down, and one more face up.

Jimmy Johnson and Louis the Pantryman both had a queen, the highest card showing. "First queen bets." The Bo's'n looked at Jimmy Johnson.

"50 cents while I look." Jimmy tossed a couple of quarters into the pot.

The betting got heavy. The two Pantrymen dropped out after paying a lot of money to look at the three more cards. I was glad that I got out early. By the last card dealt, the only ones left were the Bo's'n and Phil, the 4-8 AB.

"Dollar while I look." Phil was still high and tossed a dollar bill into the middle of the table before looking at his last card.

"It's going to cost you another double sawbuck to see my hand, Phil." The Bo's'n tossed in a $20 bill.

"You ain't got a straight or a flush, Benny, and I ain't gonna to let you buy it." The AB also tossed in another $20, followed by a $10 bill. "I'll raise you another sawbuck, seeing as how you're throwing your money away."

The Bo's'n hesitated. If both of them had straights, the AB had higher cards and would win. I guessed the Bo's'n didn't have a flush because that would beat even an ace-high straight. "Call." The Bo's'n threw in a $10 bill from his almost-gone pile of money.

Phil turned over his hole cards: king, jack and a 9. "Three jacks." Another combination was 8-9-10-jack. The queens were all dealt. The AB had been paying big bucks to hope for a 7. His only hope now was that the Bo's'n was bluffing.

"5-high straight." The Bo's'n turned over his cards and raked in well over $100. "Jimmy's deal." He slapped what was left of the deck in front of the Jimmy Johnson, who collected the rest of the cards. The other 4-8 AB, Phil, got up and left the table. The Second Cook and Baker, who'd been watching the game, took his place.

I realized then that I was in a high-stakes game—over my head, financially-speaking. I couldn't compete, when it came to bluffing, and needed to drop out from the betting quickly unless I had a pat hand.

"Five-card draw, jacks or better to open." Jimmy Johnson threw in a quarter and started to deal.

The Bo's'n bought that hand.

It was Paul's deal. "Seven-card," he announced while throwing out cards.

I finally had a hand, with two kings for hole cards and a deceptive 6 showing. I threw in a quarter to match the opening bet, "and a dollar more to play," I said. Everyone stayed in.

My next card was a 6! That gave me two pair with the first four cards. "Pair of 6s bets," Paul said.

"Three bucks to play." I decided to try to keep players in until the pot got bigger. My strategy worked for the Baker and the Pantrymen, but the Bo's'n and both ABs folded. The next card dealt by Paul didn't seem to help anyone. I got a 9. The Baker had ace-4-5 showing—a long-shot inside straight possible, but the cards shown by the Pantrymen were pitiful. I decided to keep them in the game and pretend I only had one pair. "Another three bucks." It worked and they all stayed in.

The next card was no visible aid to anyone, again. I bet $2 to try to squeeze a little more money out of the players remaining. It might have worked, except the Baker said, "$10 to play." His last card was a jack. He must have paired up and thought he could beat a pair of 6s. Both Pantrymen folded. I put in another $8 and called. Paul dealt the last card face down.

I got a 7. It was two pair—kings and 6s—for me. Unless the Baker had some pretty incredible hole cards, there was no way he could beat my hand. "I'll go $3 again." I wanted a little more of the Baker's money.

"And, again, you must pay $10 to play this game."

"Call." I threw in almost all of my money. Only $2.50 was left.

The Baker turned over his cards. "Pair of jacks." I flipped over my kings—I didn't even need the second pair—and raked in the pot. I'd more than doubled my money and now had more than $60. I figured that was enough to weather the heavy betting I was expecting from the Bo's'n, Jimmy Johnson and others in the deck department. I didn't realize how heavily they would bet.

It was the Saloon Pantryman's turn to deal. "Five-card draw." Jimmy Johnson bet heavily, forcing the faint of heart to fold after drawing cards. I had three 10s but lost my nerve when the bet came around to me at $31. Everyone else folded except my Pantryman, Paul, who bet everything he had in front of him, which was one dollar more than he needed—allowing a token raise.

"Here's another dollar, Pantryman, let's see what you've got." Paul turned over a hand with a pair of kings. "I've got you beat with my openers," Jimmy Johnson sneered, turning over two aces. He didn't show his other three cards.

It was the Bo's'n's deal again. Paul said he had no more money left and started to leave the table. "You want a draw on the Poker Book, Pantryman?" Jimmy Johnson said he could sign for $50 and pay it back when the crew got a draw against their wages in the next port.

"$50? Sure." Jimmy Johnson pulled out a small black notebook, made a notation and handed it to Paul. After my Pantryman signed, Jimmy pulled $50 out of his pile and gave it to him. Paul stayed in the game.

The Bo's'n dealt seven-card stud again. The Baker lost the last of his money on that hand.

"Want to sign the Poker Book?" Jimmy Johnson asked in a slightly taunting manner.

"No." The Baker stood up and left the rec room.

The Saloon Pantryman was the second player to sign Jimmy Johnson's Poker Book. While the Saloon Pantryman signed, the Baker's seat was taken by Jimmie Singleton, one of the ABs on the 8-12, who was on gangway watch when I joined the Del Valle. The 8-12 evening deck watch was split into three segments of one hour and 20 minutes each by the two ABs and one Ordinary Seaman. During each segment, one of the watchstanders was at the wheel, steering the ship; one was on the bow, as Lookout, and one was on Standby. The one on Standby was to stand by for emergencies or for when an extra hand was needed, and to make coffee and call the next watch out of their bunks. Or, as in the case of Jimmie Singleton, the Standby could get paid for playing poker for an hour and twenty minutes while on watch.

"Five-card stud," I said when it was my turn to deal.

Jimmy Johnson bet heavily and forced everyone out except me by the time there was only one more card to deal. "It'll cost you $40 to get your last card, Messman." He put two $20 bills into the pot. $40 was all the money I had and he knew it.

I had a king-jack-10 showing with an ace in the hole. It was a good hand for five-card stud, where even low pairs are infrequent. Jimmy

Johnson had an ace-queen-6 showing. I thought he was bluffing about having a queen in the hole and was trying to scare me out of calling his bet. If he was, my ace-king would beat his ace-queen for high cards. "I'll call." I put all my money in the middle of the table and then dealt the last card, face up.

The last card didn't visibly help either one of us. I got a 6 and the AB got a 4. I was all in and couldn't place a bet. "Check."

"I call your check, Messman."

"Ace-king-jack." I turned over my ace.

Jimmy Johnson turned over his. "Pair of queens."

It was my turn to sign the Poker Book.

Jimmie Singleton went back on watch. His chair was taken by the 4-8 Oiler, Floyd Smith. The only thing I remember about Floyd was that he was an older fellow, likely pushing 60. He didn't last long in that game. I should have gotten out too, but I was obsessed with calling Jimmy Johnson on a bluff. The two Pantrymen stayed in, each drawing another $50 on the Poker Book. Even with heavy betting from Jimmy Johnson and his pals in the deck department, I managed to stretch out my $50 advance until 2300 hours when I got up to head for my rack.

The poker game went on the next night and every night after that, starting at 2000 hours. I had some good hands, and won an occasional pot, but I never won huge pots like Jimmy Johnson, Ruffner, and the Bo's'n did. The limit on advances from the Poker Book was $50 at a time. That meant that when I had a good hand, I didn't have enough money to match the serious bettors and would have to go all in before the betting stopped. Paul and Louis the Pantrymen got a few more advances on the Poker Book and then quit playing. They were replaced by various Oilers and Firemen, the Wiper, and Ordinary Seamen.

Like a fool, I kept playing. I don't know whether or not Jimmy Johnson had any control over the cards being dealt. I do know that every time we went one-to-one—usually when I was all in—he had a better hand than I did. By the time we reached Panama I was into the Poker Book for a month's wages that I had yet to earn. That meant that in every port I'd have to pay half my draw on wages to the Poker Book. I finally quit playing.

The SS Del Valle arrived at the Port of Cristobal, Panama in the wee hours of May 12, 1970. My ship went right into the Panama Canal and no one got a chance to go ashore in the adjacent city of Colon, even if they'd wanted to. It took 10 hours to transit the 50 miles across Panama. After I set up for breakfast I went on deck and looked at dense jungle as we were pulled through the Canal by an electric locomotive.

Jimmie Singleton, the 8-12 AB, was my first customer for breakfast. He told me that the Panama Canal had three sets of locks and artificial lakes to take us up across the Isthmus of Panama separating the Atlantic and Pacific Oceans. "We go up and down less than 100 feet in elevation when going across Panama," he said. "We'll stop in Balboa at the end to take on bunkers. That'll be our last chance to go ashore until the Philippines." Balboa was on the Pacific side of Panama and was in the U.S.-owned Canal Zone, which extended five miles each way north and south of the Canal itself. We stopped at a fuel dock there after lunch was over. During lunch, the crew had been talking excitedly about a cathouse in Panama City just north of the Canal Zone.

The Captain announced a draw that morning. The crew lined up outside the Captain's office to be handed cash advances against wages. At the end of the line, waiting with the Poker Book, was Jimmy Johnson. After half my draw went to the Poker Book, there was enough left, I figured, to get laid.

Other than groping around in the back seat of cars with girls at drive-in movies, I didn't have much sexual experience. If dry-humping doesn't count, I was technically a virgin. I eagerly joined Jimmie Singleton and some others in the crew to go ashore in Balboa to visit the cathouse.

There was a tall fence separating the U.S. Canal Zone from the rest of Panama. While waiting for a taxi to the cathouse, I remember seeing Panamanians with angry faces glaring through the fence.

The cathouse was a large ranch-style hacienda with a broad veranda. Inside was a long bar with lots of friendly women. I don't remember much about that afternoon and can't even describe the woman I ended up with. All I remember is that I couldn't get it up.

One of the Oilers told me that we took on better than a thousand barrels (almost 50,000 gallons) of fuel in Balboa. A new Second Electrician—Robert Tyler—joined the ship there. It was still the 12th of

May when the SS Del Valle cast off from Balboa to enter the Gulf of Panama and start steaming for the Philippines.

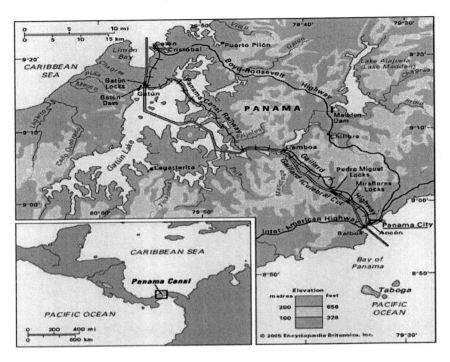

The next day, after cleaning the messhall when dinner was over, I went to the rail on the starboard side just forward of the house. I pulled out a cigarette and stared at the horizon while a slight breeze blew through my hair. "I'm not a man," I thought, re-living my humiliation with the prostitute in Panama City. "Am I queer?" Idle thoughts of throwing myself over the rail percolated into my brain. "I don't even have the guts to kill myself." I'd tried to commit suicide twice, both when I was 15 years old. The first time was in New Hampshire. I'd inexpertly bought 32-caliber ammunition for the 7-mm German pistol I'd found in an old trunk of my father's WWII memorabilia. The bullets fit, but when I put the pistol to the side of my head and pulled the trigger, it jammed.

The second time was during a visit to the apartment of my eldest sister in Cambridge, Massachusetts, near Harvard Square. This time I had a ceremonial Korean dagger and intended to stick it into my stomach. I sat over the toilet so I wouldn't mess up my sister's

38

apartment. I pulled up my shirt and placed the tip of the dagger just above my belly button. And then I lost my nerve. "I can't do this," I thought. I realized that I didn't have the courage to commit suicide.

I remembered those episodes and decided that rather than throwing myself into the Pacific Ocean I'd go back to my fo'c'sle to read.

The SS Del Valle was overloaded and wallowed rather than rolled in the gentle Pacific swells. It would take us a month to reach our destination of Saigon. There would be no land in sight until a couple of days before that—four weeks after leaving Balboa—when we stopped for fuel in the Philippines. The weather was warm and pleasant, and save for an occasional storm, the seas calm. Our route was straight across the Pacific, just north of the equator, passing below Hawaii and above Polynesia.

The poker game continued every night—without me—starting at 2000 hours. The Poker Book rules were that I had to give at least half of every draw to Jimmy Johnson. The crew was allowed to draw only against their base wages, not overtime, so it was going to take me most of the voyage to pay off what I owed on the Poker Book.

I got to work overtime occasionally in the afternoons, cleaning and arranging the storerooms, or sougeeing (wiping with cloth and cleanser) the messhall bulkheads (walls).

The young guys would have to fight off seasickness during those times when we did hit rough weather. I got a little queasy but never barfed, thanks to having gotten seasick once at an early age. One of the Ordinaries, Malvin Jerkins, told the first-trippers how to avoid puking. "Just light a joint and jump up off the deck when the ship is at its highest point, and then see how long you can stay in the air while the ship drops down into the next trough." It seemed to work. Malvin was 18—a lanky lad from Pensacola, Florida. The Del Valle was his second ship. I don't think he was worried about seasickness, but I saw him frequently on the fantail testing out his antidote.

The days dragged on as we lumbered our way across the Pacific at 15 knots. First the fresh milk ran out. The substitute canned milk tasted foul to me even when put into strong, bad coffee. The crew called it "Paul Hall milk" after the current President of the SIU. I heard that the moniker stemmed from some long-ago strike he led, while still young and feisty, over requisite shipboard provisions during the early days of the union. Every morning at breakfast I dutifully placed a one-quart metal can of Paul Hall milk on each table so it could be added to a bowl of boxed cereal for those of my customers who really needed to have that as part of their diet.

After the real milk, the fresh vegetables ran out and then the fresh fruit. Tempers started to get short. It got worse when the booze ran out. Prime rib was a specialty served for Sunday dinner. One Sunday Jimmy Johnson told me his prime rib was too rare. I took the plate back to galley.

"Motherfucker!" J.C. slapped the stainless steel serving table hard with the blade of a French knife. He grabbed a spatula and scooped up the prime rib, tossing it onto the cast-iron stovetop. He let it cook for one second, flipped it over to cook for one second more, and then tossed it back onto the plate. "If that cracker sends his food back again I'll put some crouton oil in it!" I took the plate back to the messhall.

"The Chief Cook put your prime rib back on the stove. He says you're going to have to come talk to him if you want it more well done than this." Jimmy Johnson looked at the still-medium prime rib, then stood up and left the messhall cursing under his breath.

"What's crouton oil," I asked the Third Cook after I carried Jimmy Johnson's uneaten plate to the pantry and went into the galley for another order.

"It's what'll make you shit so fast you can't make it to the head," Harry told me. "That AB don't want to fuck with J.C."

The Third Cook tipped me off that it was also the Pantryman's job to make cold drinks, not just the Messman's. Harry told me this when we were still in the Gulf of Mexico. I confronted Paul with this information and told him that I'd compromise and prepare the cold drinks every other day. Preparing the cold drinks consisted of getting ice for three aluminum pitchers for each of the four tables, filling them with Kool-aid, iced tea, and ice water and then carrying them from the pantry to the messhall. It took no more than five minutes. That arrangement worked fine until we crossed the dateline.

The ship's clocks got retarded one hour about every three days as we steamed west across time zones. On those days, during the nighttime, each of the three deck department watches would move the messhall and galley clocks backwards 20 minutes. That meant the deck and engine departments had to work 20 minutes longer on each nighttime watch while the steward department got to sleep an hour longer. When we crossed the date line, in the middle of the Pacific Ocean, we skipped a calendar day and everyone got paid for a day they hadn't worked. It would work in reverse on the way back when steaming east. The same calendar day would be repeated and everyone had to work the same day twice while only getting paid for one day.

"It's your turn to make the cold drinks," Paul said at 1030 while we were in the crew pantry starting to prepare for lunch.

"No it's not. I made them yesterday." I had put out canned juice and Paul Hall milk for breakfast, so the drinks hadn't been an issue earlier.

"Today's the 29th. That's an odd number. Our deal is that I make the cold drinks on even dates and you make them on odd dates." My Pantryman was getting militant about Kool-Aid, water, and iced tea.

"We crossed the dateline. BFD. I'm not making cold drinks two days in a row. The (SIU) contract says that's your job, too. Do you think I just fell off a turnip cart?" I hadn't even thought about what would happen two days later on May 31st and June 1st, both odd-numbered dates.

Paul glared at me. I went into the messhall while he sullenly lined up the aluminum pitchers.

I got my tables all ready to go before the early arrivals on the 12-4 watch started coming in. I was leaning on the stainless steel serving table in the galley, bullshitting with J.C. and the Third Cook, when Paul walked in. I glanced at the clock on the port bulkhead and saw that it read 1120, time to expect some customers. I pushed myself upright, turned toward the messhall, and walked right into a Sunday punch. Whack! Without saying a word, Paul had swung his right arm wide and around to my face. I had only enough time to turn away to the right, when his fist hit me so hard on the left cheek that it knocked me down. Paul turned and walked out of the galley while I lay stunned on the red tile floor. "Nothing's broken," I thought while I felt my face. There was a bit of blood and my cheekbone was numb. J.C. and the Third Cook watched as I picked myself off the deck.

"Don't do anything stupid, John," the Third Cook said. Harry must have seen the fire in my eyes as I started toward the pantry. "You'll be losing your papers if you fight on a ship. Don't go topside on him, neither. You got to wait until he's down the gangway and you be on the beach." He was right. I was on my way to get even with Paul but paused to think about what Harry was telling me.

'Going topside' meant turning my Pantryman in to the Captain. I was trained not to squeal on my equals while growing up—even more so in high school. Instead I started scheming about how I was going to lay for him on shore once we got to Viet Nam: even though the Pantryman was wider than me, I had a wiry strength and was quicker. I figured I could take him. Paul and I gave each other a wide berth while working lunch that day.

"Are you going to make the cold drinks today?" Paul asked me in a threatening tone at lunch two days later on the second-in-a-row odd day.

"Hell no! After that sucker punch—are you kidding? It's your job anyway. I was willing to help you out before, but not now." Paul sulked his way through lunch, glaring daggers, and made implied threats about beating the crap out of me. It got so I was afraid to have my back turned when he was anywhere close.

I decided this situation couldn't be allowed to go on until I caught him on land. "Hey Paul," I said as we finished up after dinner that evening, "I'll make you a deal. If you can beat me at arm wrestling I'll go back to making the cold drinks on odd days."

"Let's go!" Paul said without hesitation, apparently confident that his 60-70 pound weight advantage would assure easy victory.

After both of us finished mopping, we sat opposite each other at one of the small messhall tables. Louis, the Saloon Pantryman, walked in from his pantry and was the only spectator. Paul and I each extended our right forearms on the table and grasped hands. Each of our left hands was then positioned palm-down on the table to hold the other's elbow in place. "I'm going to count to three and we'll start," I said. "One, two, three—go!" We both strained as hard as we could, our faces turning beet-red. Being a bit taller than my Pantryman, my arm was at an angle slightly less perpendicular to the table surface than his. Added to his advantage was the fact that my Pantryman's forearm was half again as thick as mine.

It was no contest. After about 20 seconds of straining against each other, I slowly bent Paul's arm half an inch to his right. My dominance increased as I pressed his arm further to the right. At 45 degrees Paul's resistance snapped and I slammed his arm on the table. I was stronger than my Pantryman and now we both knew it. The look in my eye said it all: "Don't fuck with me, Paul!" and I didn't have to actually say it out loud. What I did say was, "I tell you what, Paul. Even though you lost, I'll give you a break and still make the cold drinks every other day."

I didn't have any more trouble with my Pantryman after that.

Behavior by some in the crew got strange as we steamed ever farther west with no sight of land. There were fire and boat drills every week during which the crew ran out all the hoses to prepare for imaginary fires on deck and then lowered the lifeboats half way to the water before ratcheting them back up. It was rote and routine but one afternoon the 4-8 Fireman, John Miller, simply refused to get out of his rack to participate. I don't know what he was thinking. It was bad enough that the Captain put his misdeed in the logbook and docked him a day's pay ($15.68), but he would certainly have to talk to the Coast Guard when we returned to the U.S. According to the Third Cook, the Coast Guard would suspend the Fireman's seaman's papers for some amount of time—or even revoke them if he had a bad record—as punishment for missing a fire and boat drill.

My Pantryman shared a fo'c'sle with Bill Greenwalt, the Saloon Messman. Greenwalt was an odd duck and I didn't have much to do with him. Only a year older than me, he was prematurely balding and had a slight paunch. Rumor had it that he was the son of a doctor from somewhere in the Midwest who pulled strings to get his son in the merchant marine for a draft deferment. Greenwalt didn't seem to have much in the way of muscle but he did have a large Bowie knife that he loved to play with. I figured that my Pantryman and Greenwalt deserved each other and idly wondered what spawn would issue if they bred. I wouldn't see the depth of Greenwalt's psychological problems until we reached the Philippines.

Once a week the crew got to buy things from the slop chest. The equivalent of a small store, run by the Steward, it was where we could buy basics like toothpaste, deodorant, or soda. The Judge ran sales from the slop chest when the Steward didn't feel like it. The most popular items for sale were cartons of duty-free cigarettes at $2.50 each. The limit was two cartons each per week. Jimmie Singleton, the 8-12 AB, told me that Winston cigarettes could be traded for liquor or women in the Philippines. I only smoked about one pack per day of Lucky Strike and already had a good supply of those, so I started stocking up on Winstons. I had four cartons in my locker by the time we arrived in the Philippines.

On June 9th we anchored in Bataan harbor to take on bunkers. Bataan is on the island of Luzon, on the other side of the bay from Manila to the east, and just south of Subic Bay. Less than 30 years earlier it had been the location of the last stand against the Japanese invasion of the Philippines. After the Americans and Filipinos surrendered, the Bataan Death March started there in 1942. U.S. Army General Douglas MacArthur got out before the surrender and gave a speech in Australia promising, "I shall return."

One of the Oilers told me later that we took on 6500 barrels of oil —a little over 25,000 gallons. We weren't there long and I didn't go ashore, but Greenwalt, the Saloon Messman, did.

A flotilla of bum boats—various wooden craft, 20 to 50 feet in length and powered by oar, sail, or motor—surrounded the Del Valle to barter for anything a sailor could possibly desire. The going rate, I soon found out, was that one carton of American cigarettes was worth a fifth of liquor or a case of San Miguel beer. Two cartons of cigarettes would buy a short time with a woman. The Filipinos in the bum boats threw ropes with grappling hooks 20 feet up to any open porthole where a seaman stuck his head out willing to barter. I wasn't too sure how to go about pulling up a woman and wondered how I'd get her through the porthole, even if I could get it up this time. And there was the Judge to think about during any quickie date I might have. Instead, I decided to stock up on liquor. I threw down four cartons of Winston and pulled up two cases of San Miguel and two fifths of rum in exchange.

While I was hauling up the cases of beer to my porthole, some of my shipmates were on deck, forward of the house, making wholesale purchases of booze in large quantity. After I finished my trading, I poked my head out from the starboard passageway to watch the show on the main deck. I didn't see any women being pulled aboard, but perhaps 10 of my shipmates were bringing alcohol onto the open deck as fast as they could haul it up. The Master of the ship put a stop to that. Captain Erling Hansen was in his mid-50s and about my size. At dusk that evening, right after I started watching from the house, he appeared with a .45 pistol strapped to his waist and swaggered forward on the plank atop the ARVN tanks and trucks on deck. "They'll be no grog on my ship!" he yelled, and loudly ordered the Bo's'n and the Day Man (AB Maintenance on the day watch) to cut all lines to the bum boats that weren't cast off. When giving this order, the Captain slurred his words slightly and sounded to me like he was drunk. My shipmates at the rail rapidly completed or cut short their transactions.

Late that night, just before we finished fueling, Greenwalt was brought back to the ship by a Filipino harbor security guy in plain clothes. There were murky rumors about the Saloon Messman having pulled a knife on a prostitute. What was known was that Greenwalt had pulled his Bowie knife on the security guy who brought him back to the ship. The security guy pulled out a gun in response, so that wasn't much of a standoff. For reasons I don't understand, the security guy gave Greenwalt his knife back after bringing him back aboard.

On June 11th the SS Del Valle steamed from the Philippines into the South China Sea. That marked our entry into the war zone and the start of a 100% bonus on base wages. With the booze taken aboard at Bataan, it also marked the start of party-time!

"Did you hear about the Columbia Eagle?" Malvin Jerkins, the 4-8 Ordinary, asked me. We were both sitting on the bottom bunk in the fo'c'sle shared by my Pantryman and Greenwalt, the Saloon Messman. My Pantryman, Paul, sat at an angle to us in the chair for the desk. We were all holding 12-ounce bottles of San Miguel beer. A fifth of rum, two-thirds full, stood on the desk in front of Paul.

"That was an SIU ship on the same run as us, wasn't it?" I responded. "I heard something about a mutiny, right after I started working at the New Orleans hall. What happened?"

"I heard about that too," Paul added. "It was just three months ago, in March. The Eagle was a Victory ship with an SIU crew, owned by Columbia Steamship Company. She was under MSTS (Military Sea Transportation Service) charter, carrying napalm bombs for one of our air bases in Thailand. A couple of commies in the unlicensed crew tried to turn the ship and all the bombs over to the reds running Cambodia. It was the first mutiny aboard an American ship in 150 years."

45

"That's not the way I heard it," the 4-8 Ordinary replied. "I heard that two heads in the crew got tired of getting harassed by the World War II alcoholics running the ship. The BR and a Fireman pulled guns and put the old farts off in lifeboats. They docked the Eagle in Cambodia the next day. The SIU wants to hush this up because it was our union brothers who mutinied."

Greenwalt entered the fo'c'sle, grabbed a beer from a bucket full of ice and San Miguel and sat next to me on the bottom bunk. Malvin Jerkins continued. "The CIA engineered a change in government right after that, getting rid of the Prince of Cambodia. The two heads disappeared into the jungle. I don't know what happened to the other 13 guys who stayed on the Eagle with the mutineers." Greenwalt got up, took a slug from the bottle of rum, then sat back down and started playing with his Bowie knife. He fondled the knife like he was playing with his dick.

"I'm telling you," Malvin wrapped up his story, "if the old fuckers hadn't messed with the young guys on the Columbia Eagle there probably would never have been a mutiny. They were probably minding their own business, smoking dope on the fantail, just like we do.

"What's this 'we' shit, Jerkins?" Greenwalt dragged the blade of his knife across his thumb to test its sharpness.

"You should try some, Bill," my Pantryman, Paul, said to Greenwalt. "It might mellow you out so you'd stop fucking around with that knife."

"I'll show you how I'm going to fuck around with this knife when you're in the rack." Greenwalt slept in the lower bunk and Paul had the upper one. Greenwalt lay back on his bunk and with his knife started thrusting at the bottom of the Paul's mattress between the bed coils. I felt a bit nervous being so close to Greenwalt and that Bowie knife and stood up. The Ordinary stayed where he was at the head of the bunk and seemed entertained by Greenwalt's destruction of Paul's mattress. Then Louis, the Saloon Pantryman, walked in. He bunked in the Third Cook's foc'c'sle.

"Hey Louis," I said, "want a beer?" I didn't know what the chemistry was between Greenwalt and his Pantryman in the saloon, but I was happy with the distraction that Louis provided.

"Sure." Louis jumped up on the top bunk.

Greenwalt tired of destroying Paul's mattress and got up to take another slug of rum. "Hey, Sambo," Greenwalt grabbed Louis and pulled him off the bunk, "ever eaten yellow pussy?"

"You a crazy motherfucker!" Louis wrestled free and left the fo'c'sle. Greenwalt turned around to the glares of Paul, the 4-8 Ordinary, and me.

"I was just playing with him!" Greenwalt said defiantly. "I gotta piss." He went down the passage toward the head.

Greenwalt came back into the fo'c'sle a few minutes later and sat down on the bottom bunk. "Where's my knife?" No one answered. "Goddammit!" Greenwalt started violently pulling the covers off his bunk. "There's going to be trouble if I don't find that knife," he said ominously. He got an empty beer bottle from the trash can and started filling it with lighter fluid. Then he stuffed some toilet paper into the neck, squirted more lighter fluid on it, and grabbed Paul's Zippo lighter off the desk. He lit the toilet paper at the top of the bottle. "I'm going to kill all three of you, and the Steward, too." Greenwalt sprang to the open porthole. He put his arm out, holding the flaming beer bottle. "Where's my knife?" No one answered. Greenwalt threw his miniature Molotov cocktail against the hull of the Del Valle. Nothing happened. The beer bottle must have bounced off the side of the ship, without breaking, and plopped into the South China Sea.

"You're sick, Greenwalt." Paul stood up to get away from him.

"And you're going to die," Greenwalt shot back, "as soon as you go to sleep in that bunk." Malvin Jerkins, Paul, and I hurriedly left and went up to the messhall. Greenwalt followed us.

The poker game had gotten smaller, as more and more in the crew were parted from their money. The game had so few players left that it was played at a smaller table in the starboard, aft corner of the messhall. It was now the sharks, mostly in the deck department, feeding on themselves.

Malvin, Paul, and I started to play a game of Hearts when Greenwalt came in and went to the messhall blackboard. He put swastikas at the edges with chalk and then wrote, "The three grass smokers beware."

Those were fighting words, given the times. The older guys in the crew knew that most of the new generation smoked pot and, even though they didn't approve, usually looked the other way. My

Pantryman, however, was a bit older and a Navy veteran; he was supposed to know better. Greenwalt was outing him. "Don't be saying that shit about me, Greenwalt!"

"Want to fight, Paul?" Greenwalt went into what he thought was a martial arts stance. Paul left the messhall.

I don't remember how that night ended but I do remember the next day. When I woke up at 0600, Paul was sleeping on the deck next to the Judge's bunk in my fo'c'sle. Paul got up and told the Steward, and then the Captain, what had happened the night before. The Saloon Pantryman had to set up for breakfast by himself because Greenwalt was too hung over to get out of his rack. The Chief Mate, the Bo's'n, and the Steward were sent down to roust Greenwalt and inspect Paul's mattress. When confronted about the mattress, Greenwalt said that both he and Paul were responsible for the knife thrusts.

Captain Hansen didn't know whom to believe, between Greenwalt and Paul, and logged them both for destruction of the mattress—along with a fine of $25 each.

The Captain also ordered that the lockers of all messmen be searched for alcohol. Liquor is technically forbidden on U.S.-flagged merchant ships but, as I was soon to learn, that rule was enforced selectively. After breakfast the Steward, Chief Mate, and the Bo's'n appeared in my fo'c'sle and I was ordered to open my locker. Benny the Bo's'n hauled away my two cases of beer and both jugs of rum. I'd lost my entire stash! Benny told me later that he'd been ordered to take it up to the Captain's stateroom, rather than throw it overboard.

By the time all my booze was confiscated, we were steaming up the Long Tau River in the Republic of Viet Nam. Greenwalt never found his knife.

The messmen weren't the only ones partying after Bataan. The Second Electrician, Robert Tyler, got logged eight different times over the next few weeks for being too drunk to stand his watch. Normally the maximum one could be fined was a day's pay ($22.66 for him) but he managed to get himself logged twice on the same day, getting fined twice as much as what he would have earned had he worked that day. One day the Second Electrician was logged the first time for not turning to in the morning, and then logged again for threatening the Chief Engineer after he finally got out of his rack to look for a drink.

Even the Bo's'n got logged for being too drunk to stand his watch —but that was later, after we'd left Viet Nam.

The Captain had earlier announced a draw on wages that could be taken the afternoon of June 4th, when we were still far away from any port. That day at breakfast Jimmie Singleton the AB was my first customer, in early before his 8-12 watch. "Why's the Old Man putting out a draw when we're in the middle of the ocean?" I asked Jimmie.

"He's doing us a favor," the AB said. "Once we enter the war zone greenbacks are illegal and all you can draw is scrip."

"What's that?"

"MPC (Military Payment Certificate) or red dollars. The official exchange rate between MPC and dong (Vietnamese piastres) is lousy. The last time I was over here a $1 MPC note was only worth 100 dong. You can get a lot more dong for real dollars on the black market. Just don't get caught bringing greenbacks ashore or you could end up in an Army stockade. Gimme two eggs over easy, grits, potatoes and toast."

"Why do we have to use MPC instead of real money?" I persisted before leaving with his order.

"I dunno. Maybe they're worried that greenbacks traded on the black market will end up in the hands of Charlie (Viet Cong) who will use the money to buy more mortars. I gotta relieve the wheel at 0745."

"OK. Sorry, Jimmie." I walked quickly to the galley to put in his order.

That afternoon I drew $110 against my wages, the maximum I was allowed. I had to give half of it to Jimmy Johnson's Poker Book but still had a good stash of U.S. dollars for Saigon.

The next draw after that was June 12th when we were in the war zone and allowed to receive only military scrip. I drew $10. Jimmy Johnson wasn't particular about how he collected for the Poker Book and I handed him a $5 MPC bill outside the Captain's office.

It got hotter the closer we got to Viet Nam. Once we were there it was about 90 degrees Fahrenheit, but the humidity must have been 100%, making it very uncomfortable. I went out on deck to cool off after we entered the Long Tau River from the South China Sea. That was a pretty stupid thing to do because Jimmie Singleton told me there were Viet Cong snipers along the banks of the river. I looked out at thick jungle. The humidity was just as bad on deck as it was in my fo'c'sle and I was soon driven back inside by a short but torrential rainstorm. The heat and humidity sapped my strength and it was hard to sleep. It took a few days before I adapted and didn't feel muggy and drowsy all the time.

On June 12th, a couple of hours after entering the river, we docked at a U.S. Army base on the Long Tau in Saigon. The Del Valle was in a line of three freighters moored port side to the dock. The Army base was a sprawling affair of tents and temporary tin-roofed buildings. As soon as the gangway was lowered, American soldiers with M-16 rifles came aboard to guard the ship.

After I finished cleaning up from lunch, I went on deck to bullshit with the soldiers and find out about going ashore. The guard assigned to the top of the gangway was a black Spec. 4 (Specialist 4th Class) from North Carolina, not much older than me. "How do I get off this base to check out Saigon?"

"You gots to talk to the MPs (Military Police) at the main gate," he gestured, "and show your ID. They might search you so don't you be taking no real money with you. And you best be careful about cowboys."

"Cowboys?"

"Yeah, cowboys," the soldier said. "They be Viet Cong sympathizers in Saigon."

"I thought the South Vietnamese are our allies...?"

"Some of them are—the ones we pay money to—some of the time."

I wondered who we were fighting this war for. "What do cowboys do?"

"Well, le's see. What do they do? Two days ago there was one of yo' friends from that ship," he pointed to the freighter tied up in front of us, "and another one in back," he jerked his thumb at another C-2 docked behind the Del Valle, "who passed through the main gate. They both got they necks sliced open before a taxi could pick them up."

I thanked the soldier but decided to go ashore anyway. I figured the two seamen who got their throats cut were probably flabby, out-of-shape guys who were flashing around their money and not paying attention. After a month at sea, wild horses couldn't have kept me on the Del Valle. I grabbed my $5 MPC note and went down the gangway.

Outside the main gate was a trashy neighborhood of huts and small businesses catering to GIs. First, before going through the gate, I went to an authorized money changer and got 500 Vietnamese piastres for the $5 MPC.

All the people looked really small. As soon as I crossed the first intersection I was immediately surrounded by a dozen little kids begging for chewing gum and money. They grabbed my hands and pleaded with sorrowful dark eyes. I thought it was cute at first, even though I didn't have any gum and wasn't going to give them my dong. More and more hands started pulling on mine, then other hands started going into my pockets. I freaked out. Ripping loose from all the grasping hands, I balled my own hands into fists and started whirling around like a lateral windmill to get all those kids away from me. Looking back, after I'd been in Viet Nam for a while, I realized that those little kids were actually teenagers.

As I wandered farther away from the base I noticed more and more signs in French. Viet Nam had been a colony of France until 16 years earlier when the French were run off. I found a little bistro in an alley of shanty huts and ordered a Vietnamese beer. The proprietor didn't speak English so I communicated with a combination of sign language and pigeon French—the little I could remember from first-year French in high school. After that I went back to my ship to prepare for dinner.

On June 14th, the Del Valle steamed upriver a couple of miles to unload our cargo of tanks and trucks at the Newport docks. The Newport docks were in another heavily fortified Army garrison near the Newport Bridge across the river. The Viet Cong had tried to blow up that bridge during the Tet Offensive 18 months earlier. That's where we stayed until June 21st.

"That guard at the gangway has the strongest weed I've ever smoked!" Rick said excitedly during his afternoon coffee break the day we tied up to the Newport docks. He came to my fo'c'sle when I was off between lunch and dinner. "He called it 'dew.'" Rick Hamilton was the 12-4 Ordinary Seaman and had become my best friend on the Del Valle. He was skinny and a little taller than me, with black hair and scraggly sideburns that he was trying to grow down to his jaw. He had a moustache and goatee that were even more scraggly. Rick was from Baytown, Texas and had joined the ship in Beaumont. Like me, he was

18 and on his first ship. Also like me, he caught the Del Valle a few days too late for a draft deferment and was classified I-A. Unlike me, he didn't have a B-book in the SIU and held the lowest union seniority, a C-card.

"He gave me a fat lid for $5 MPC. Look at it!" Rick pulled out a plastic sandwich bag filled with dark-green marijuana, heavy and pungent.

"Wow!" I said after smelling Rick's stash.

"C'mon, man, let's go get laid!" Rick pulled out a $20 bill—real money—from his pocket. "The guard said there're lots of girls on Tu Do Street, and we can get better than double the official exchange rate on the black market if we have greenbacks."

"What if we get caught?" I asked.

"We won't if we stick the money in our underpants. The guard told me the MPs at the gate usually don't search seamen, and when they do it's only a pat-down for guns or dope."

"OK," I said, "let's go at 1830 after I finish with dinner." Rick was on the day watch, working on deck 0800-1700 when we were in port for more than 24 hours.

I swept and mopped the messhall after dinner and then went to my locker to put a real $20 bill into my underpants. Rick and I were simply waved through the gate by two MPs. We had enough dong between us for cab fare to the red light district so we didn't have to use our greenbacks yet.

Tu Do Street had some elegant stretches of hotels and French colonial buildings. It was dusk and I couldn't make out names, but I think we passed the huge U.S. Embassy. The taxi driver dropped us in the middle of a neon-lit block. Our eyes got wide as we surveyed countless bars, restaurants and massage parlors with beautiful Vietnamese women beckoning us from almost every doorway. "Holy cow!" Rick said.

"Keep your dick in your pants," I told him. "The first thing we have to do is change our money."

"You want change money?" A young Vietnamese man was right at my elbow like he'd been eavesdropping. "I give you 125 dong for MPC."

"How much for real money, greenbacks?" Rick flashed his $20 bill.

"Put that away," I hissed at Rick. "This guy's probably a cowboy. You want to get jumped?"

"Two hundred dong for dollar," the guy said.

"That's not enough," Rick responded.

"OK, for you 300 dong for dollar."

"That's a really good deal!" Rick whispered to me. He turned to the Vietnamese guy. "You have enough to change $40?"

"I got beaucoup dong." He pulled out a fat roll of 500 piastre notes.

"We go there to make trade." The guy motioned to a dead-end alley between two bars.

By the time we were at the end of the alley, there were three young Vietnamese men next to us, instead of just the one we'd dickered with, and they were acting a bit aggressive. After handing Rick my $20 bill for our share of the trade, I pulled out my trusty brown jackknife. It had a two-inch blade with a broken tip. I tossed it casually from one hand to the other, like I was an experienced knife-fighter who was keeping the cowboys guessing as to which hand their death would come from. "You're good at numbers," Rick said while handing me both $20 bills. "Make sure they don't short us on dong."

"OK," I responded. "You make sure we don't get any more company." I gestured toward the opening of the alley where several more young males had gathered to watch the exchange. "We can take these three cowboys," I handed Rick my jackknife, "but not all their buddies."

Rick went into a fighter's crouch, facing the alley entrance with my broken-bladed jackknife in his right hand. I turned to our original money-changer. "You said 300 dong per dollar. I've got $40." I waved the two $20 bills. "You show me 12,000 dong."

"OK, you see." The Vietnamese guy pulled out his wad and counted out 24 500-piastre notes in front of me, slowly and deliberately. He then rolled them up, scooped the bills down into his right palm, and put a rubber band around the roll. I gave him the two $20 bills with my left hand while grabbing the roll of dong with my right. It was at this point that I expected his two confederates to make their move and I stepped back to fight. Nothing happened.

"OK, Rick, we're good. Let's get out of here!" Rick stayed in his crouched position with the jackknife, slowly walking forward to the young Vietnamese—cowboys I assumed—at the mouth of the alley. I pressed my back against Rick's, and was also in a crouch, walking backwards to be ready lest the moneychangers became combatants.

"Hot shit! We did it!" Rick exclaimed after we were back on Tu Do Street. "Let's go have a drink!"

We had three drinks in the nearest bar, while ogling all the Vietnamese women working their trade. I only had to peel the first 500-piastre note off our wad to pay for all three rounds. Finally, a particularly attractive girl talked Rick into following her to the massage parlor next door. I went too.

There were about six girls in the massage parlor waiting for customers. I hadn't made a selection yet when the mama-san came out to take our money. "This number one girl," she said of the woman Rick was falling in love with. "She 500 dong for massage. She like you, maybe you pay more for extra." Rick's tongue was almost hanging out of his mouth. I pulled the wad of piastres out of my pocket.

"What the . . ?" I had a roll of 24 5-piastre notes rather than 500-piastre notes, a total of 120 dong. The roll of bills I'd gotten in the currency exchange had only been topped with a 500 piastre note— which we'd already spent. "What do we do now?" I showed Rick the 5-piastre notes.

Rick was crestfallen, looking back and forth between his intended masseuse and our meager finances. "Here, I give you this." He took off his wristwatch and tried to hand it to the young woman.

"No, no! No dong, no boom-boom." The mama-san stepped between Rick and his would-be date. The contents of my wad had not been lost on her.

"But, but… " Rick was stuttering and trying to force the mama-san to take his wristwatch in trade for a date. The rapid reversal of our fortunes left me too stunned to speak.

"You number 10," the mama-san said. "Didi, didi! You go now!" She pushed us toward the door and we got the bum's rush from the massage parlor.

120 dong wasn't even enough for cab fare. We had to walk back to the ship.

I'd gotten my fill of the black market. Some of the older Firemen and Oilers had no interest in going ashore in Saigon. The next day I traded a couple of them my greenbacks for their MPC scrip at par.

Rick and I wanted to go ashore again that evening. Before we did, the Day Man, Robert Birmingham, broke his ankle. The soldier at the gangway told me he was taken to the 3rd Field Hospital—a M.A.S.H. (Mobile Army Surgical Hospital). There was no reason to visit the Day Man, even if we knew how to get to the 3rd Field Hospital, so Rick and I sallied forth on June 15th, changing MPC to dong before wandering into Saigon.

That night we ended up in an opium den. Actually it was just a small, low-ceilinged house with no one in it except the elderly couple who lived there.

The mama-san stayed out of sight. Papa-san had a small gray goatee and looked sort of like Ho Chi Minh. He sat us down on pillows in the middle of the main room and lit a candle on the floor. After taking our money—it wasn't much, maybe a couple hundred dong for both of us—he pulled out a tubular pipe about the size of a long cigar. It was made of wood and had a hole near one end. Then he sat and produced a small bowl half full with a thick, dark-black gooey substance. He grabbed a piece of wood that looked like a popsicle stick, scooped up some of the black tar and scraped it across the hole in the pipe. Then from somewhere he pulled out what looked like a hat pin and held the sharp end over the candle. When the tip of the pin was red hot, he turned the pipe upside down and stuck one end in his mouth. Papa-san slowly slid the red hot pin through the black goo, up into the pipe, inhaling as he did. "Bon." He handed the pipe to Rick.

Papa-san got the end of the pin red hot again and repeated the process while Rick had the pipe in his mouth. Then it was my turn.

The pipe went around several times before papa-san scraped off the residue and pasted some more opium across the hole in the pipe. I was in a cloud, slowly bouncing off the low ceiling. I finally understood the meaning of the word nirvana.

Suddenly there was a blinding flash of light outside the house, followed by a deafening boom. I went from nirvana to shock in less than half a second. Shock turned to panic when the second mortar round landed about three seconds later. "We gotta get out of this place!" Rick and I both jumped up and burst through the low doorway.

More mortar rounds lit up the sky as we crashed through a neighborhood of wood shanties with tin roofs. There didn't seem to be much rhyme or reason to the way the little shacks were tightly crowded together, without yards, and no visible streets or alleys. We didn't know where we were but had a general sense of which way the river was. To get back to the Del Valle we made a crazed beeline, trampling fences and knocking over household ornaments in our panic to escape the mortar attack.

I'm not sure how long it took to get back to the ship. Once aboard, we stood at the rail and looked in awe as the Viet Cong mortar attack continued to light up the sky over Saigon. Even though I thought I'd almost been killed by a mortar shell, looking back I realize that the nearest round probably didn't land within 500 yards of me and Rick.

I finally got laid in Saigon. It was in a large tent not far outside the fence around the Army base at the Newport docks. Rick must have been there too but I don't remember seeing him. The tent was separated into cubicles by blankets hanging from overhead wires strung like clotheslines. The cubicle I was in had a thick mat, like a mattress, and nothing else—no furniture or plumbing. I don't remember the Vietnamese girl I was with either, other than that she was probably younger than me.

The tent-brothel must have been controlled by or received protection from U.S. soldiers. I was lying with the girl on the mat when I heard the sound of boots approaching. Through a gap beneath a hanging blanket I saw the butt of a rifle. "Oh, shit!" I thought. "Viet Cong. I'm going to get my throat slit while I'm naked!" Instead, it turned out that the boots were worn by an American G.I. who was delivering an order of "dew"—marijuana—to the next cubicle (maybe to Rick?).

When I lost my virginity, the only fireworks came from exploding mortar shells. If the ground shook when I had sex that night, it was from incoming rounds landing in Saigon.

On June 21st we left Saigon, bound for Cam Ranh Bay. The Del Valle only got hit by a single sniper's bullet that I know of, in the 20-odd miles down the Long Tau River before we were back onto salt water.

Cam Ranh Bay is on the South China Sea, north of Saigon. We got there late the next day. The Del Valle tied up at a sprawling, sandy U.S.

Air Force base. On an island in the bay was an old French fortress that looked abandoned.

We stayed in Cam Ranh Bay for two days and one night. I don't remember much about being there, probably because it was too dangerous to go off the base—and rocket attacks were common. Merchant seamen were allowed to use military facilities, like the PX (Post Exchange), Commissary, and service clubs. The only thing to do for kicks the night we were there was to go to the EM (enlisted men's) Club and drink. My fo'c'sle mate, the Judge, went to the EM Club and had one beer. It was the only time I ever saw him go ashore. I went with him.

The guy next to me at the bar in the club was a Marine, judging by his uniform. "What's a jarhead doing in a fly-boy bar," I asked him.

"Ground crew for Marine jets," he answered. "The Army and Navy also fly out of here, not just the Air Force."

"Where do they all fly to?"

"All over 'Nam, delivering supplies and going on bombing missions. This is a transportation hub. C-130s fly in supplies from Korea and the Philippines, and then we distribute it."

"What was here before this was an air base?"

"Nothing. I heard that Army Engineers bulldozed the jungle for airfields here in '65."

The Marine was wearing a flak jacket and I wasn't. I thought that was a pretty good reason to go back to the ship with the Judge, lest I got caught in another mortar attack.

On June 24th we cast off and steamed back into the South China Sea, bound for Manila. We also left the war zone and our 100% pay bonus ended.

The 100% pay bonus for 14 days, even though on base wages only —not overtime—earned me enough money to get $100 on June 25th when the Old Man put out a draw. Manila was supposed to be a good port according to Jimmie Singleton, the 8-12 AB. Half my draw went to the Poker Book but I figured I could have a pretty good time with $50.

On June 26th we tied up in Manila to take on bunkers. After Viet Nam there was quite a bit of pent-up anxiety and almost all in the crew that could went ashore during our one day in Manila. I ended up in a whorehouse/bar called Kirby Seaman Inn. I don't remember what the place looked like, nor who of my shipmates were there with me, but they probably included Rick Hamilton and Jimmie Singleton. I do remember that I was with a short, buxom and very friendly woman named Melinda and that I had a really good time. I would pay for it later.

I'd made a deal with Paul, my Pantryman, to cover dinner for me so I could have fun in Manila all afternoon and evening. Paul decided he wanted to have fun in Manila, too and pieced off two Filipinos to cover both our jobs. Filipinos worked for cheap and I understood that it was common practice to hire them to cover for seamen who went ashore in Manila to have a good time, but I found out the hard way that the practice was technically prohibited. Someone must have complained, apparently because the Filipinos working dinner hadn't made salads, and the Steward got called to the Old Man's office. The Steward had been ashore, too and not doing his job. To cover his own fat ass he threw three messmen to the wolves. My Pantryman, Louis the Saloon Pantryman and I all got logged half a day's pay ($6.07 each) for being late for dinner and not preparing salads. I don't know why Greenwalt wasn't logged, too. Maybe he had no desire to be with women without his Bowie knife and decided not to go ashore.

I was allowed to enter a written response to the accusations against me in the logbook. I wrote: "I did my duty. I did not hire a local man." That was technically true because I thought Paul was going to do my job. Paul told me that when he signed the log he wrote that he didn't know that he wasn't allowed to hire Filipinos.

The S.S. Del Valle left Manila that night, bound for Inchon, Korea. The Bo's'n, Benny Brinson, was logged a day's pay ($20.60) for being too drunk to prepare the vessel for sea.

It took us five days to reach Inchon, steaming north along the China coast. On June 28th the Old Man put out a draw—greenbacks, thank god!—and I got $85.

The 2nd Electician got logged for being drunk three days in a row. I wondered how he was going to keep his seaman's papers when we got back and he had to talk to the Coast Guard.

"What's there to do in Inchon?" I asked the 8-12 AB. Jimmie Singleton was my first customer for breakfast one day right after we'd passed Taiwan in the East China Sea en route to Korea.

"The Paradise Casino started letting Westerners in last year. There're girls there, too." Just then we hit the fist trough of a typhoon and took a hard roll. I'd placed four settings on each of four tables, with an eight-ounce water glass upside down at each place. Jimmie was sitting at one of the tables and grabbed the edge so he wouldn't get thrown out of his chair. I braced myself against the bulkhead. 16 water glasses flew off the tables and shattered on the red steel deck in unison.

I swept up the broken glass with some difficulty, as the glass fragments slid back and forth, and then somehow managed to serve breakfast. Only cold sandwiches were served for lunch because pots wouldn't stay on the galley stoves. The 12-4 Third Mate must have steered us out of the typhoon because things were back to normal before dinner.

We arrived at Inchon on July 1st. Inchon is on the west coast of Korea and is Seoul's outlet to the Yellow Sea about 20 miles away. It is best known to Americans as the site for the turning point of the Korean War. In September 1950, U.S. Marines overseen by Douglas MacArthur, then General of the Army, made a surprise landing and recaptured Seoul from the North Koreans. The Battle of Inchon served to relieve pressure on besieged U.N. forces at the very southern end of the Korean Peninsula and is generally believed to have allowed U.S. and U.N. armies to launch an offensive that went almost to the border of China. That, of course, resulted in China jumping in and U.N forces were pushed back to what is still South Korea. The Demilitarized Zone —on either side of the 38th parallel, separating North and South Korea —is just north of Seoul and Inchon.

The Del Valle docked at or near a U.S. Army base. We took on cargo of household furnishings for military families returning to the States. The first night ashore, I took $40 in greenbacks and went to the Paradise Casino.

I don't remember much about the Paradise except for bright lights and Koreans in evening dress. I headed straight for a blackjack table, a half-circle surrounded by eight stools and a dealer in the middle. Four Asian men in Western-style suits were the only ones at the table. The dealer was a man wearing what I assumed was traditional Korean garb, a kind of buttoned-up long shirt with baggy trousers. With blue jeans and a T-shirt, I stuck out like a sore thumb, and as the only Westerner at the table I got a cool reception. I didn't care. I was there to gamble.

I'd never gambled in a casino before and had to pick up the rules as I went along because they differed in small ways from the blackjack I'd known in high school. The main difference was that both of the initial two cards to each player were dealt face-down, while one of the dealer's two cards was dealt face-up. The dealer had to hit at 16 or less and had to stay at 17. It was almost impossible to count cards because the dealer shuffled after every hand.

The dealer didn't speak English and I didn't speak Korean, but the sign language for blackjack is apparently universal so I had no problem. The minimum bet was 100 won—about 25 cents. I don't remember what the maximum was but it was a lot more than I had. I played a modified system of starting with the minimum bet and then doubling it after every losing hand. It wasn't very sophisticated but with $40 (15,000 won) for a grubstake, the dealer would have to win seven or eight hands in a row to bust me. The odds against that happening were more than 100-to-1.

I was doing OK with my little system, winning slowly but steadily, when I heard a female voice over my right shoulder. "You want drink?"

I turned and saw a petite and very curvaceous young Korean woman wearing a tight red silk dress that accentuated her figure. "Drink?" My head started spinning when she smiled at me. "How much?"

"Free drink for you."

"Free? How about Jack Daniel's?" She nodded. "Black Label, on the rocks," I added. She looked confused. "It's OK," I backtracked, "Jack Daniel's with ice, good." She swayed off to the bar and I went back to the hand that'd been dealt.

I kept winning, but my stack of chips grew very slowly. Blackjack —21 with the first two cards—hands were paid at only 1.5-to-1, instead of 2-1 like in homey rules. After the curvaceous cocktail waitress brought me a second shot of Jack Daniel's, I started thinking about all the money I'd lost on the ship. "I could stay here all night and still not win as much as I've paid to the Poker Book," I thought. I upped my initial bets to 200 won. After winning a few more hands I increased my opening bet to 500 won. The money started coming in faster and my pile of chips totaled close to 50,000 won—almost $150.

I was sipping my third Jack Daniel's when the dealer had a run of luck, winning four hands in a row. By this time I had started the betting at 1,000 won. Doubling again, after four losses, meant that I had to put down 16,000 won—about $45—on the next hand. "This guy can't win again," I thought as I pushed 16 thousand-won chips up to the betting zone.

I was still looking at the next two cards I was dealt when the dealer flipped over an Ace next to the King he had showing. Blackjack! He raked in my 16 thousand-won chips.

"This is it!" I thought. I had a little more than 15,000 won left, about what I'd started with. I could walk out and chalk off the evening as free entertainment, or I could go for the gusto and try to reclaim most of my winnings. "The odds against the dealer winning six hands in a row are 32-to-1," I thought. I hesitated. The dealer looked at me expectantly. I was holding up the game. Something made me remember graffiti I once saw on the restroom wall at the Seven Seas bar in New Orleans: "Battlefields throughout the ages are littered with a thousand bleached bones of the indecisive." I pushed all my remaining chips forward into the betting zone.

The dealer had a four showing, a lousy card because chances were that the required hit would put him over 21. I had a seven and a five, a 12 hand. I should have stayed but I hesitated again. "The dealer's been awful lucky with his draws," I thought. "He'll beat me with anything he draws if he doesn't bust, and I've got nine chances out of 13 to not bust with another card." I scraped my cards on the table to request another one. It was a Jack! I had a hand totaling 22 and was busted. I stood up and slinked out of the casino.

Half-a-dozen prostitutes were loitering outside the Paradise Casino when I walked out at about 2100 hours that night. The cocktail waitress in the tight silk dress had gotten my blood up while I was playing blackjack. "I should get laid," I thought while surveying the Korean women lined up against the wall of the casino. I still had military scrip in my pocket, left over from Cam Ranh Bay. "The casino wouldn't take MPC, but these gals will," I thought. "American GIs are all over the place in Inchon." Looking for a bargain, I approached the oldest-looking woman of those assembled. She didn't speak much English but was good with numbers. We struck a bargain and walked to her place, 10 minutes away.

At the woman's apartment, I was eager to get our clothes off but she wanted to take care of business first. I pulled out my wad of military scrip. "No, no MPC!" she said. "Red dollar no good!" I got the bum's rush out of her apartment.

Taxi drivers didn't like the color of my money, either. I ended up walking back to the ship.

The next day, July 2nd, I learned that the Saloon Messman, Greenwalt, got hurt the day before. He fell while walking in Inchon, I was told. If he was to be believed, he'd hurt his left leg and hip. Greenwalt remained in his rack and the Judge took over for him in the saloon.

I went ashore to the Army base to get a newspaper during my one-hour break between breakfast and lunch. The 1970 draft lottery had been held the day before. I hoped that the Stars and Stripes, the military newspaper, would have the results.

"Oh, shit!" My birthday drew #68. According to General Hershey —former Director of the Selective Service System—young men with numbers up to 100 should expect to be drafted that year, but it could go as high as #150. "I better apply for college, pronto!" I had sent my aunt and uncle a postcard from Mobile with a mailing address for the S.S. Del Valle, c/o Delta Steamship Co., so they'd know where to send an application to the University of Washington that I'd asked them to get. It took a long time for mail to reach the ship, even for those willing to pay more than six cents regular postage to send letters by air mail. The application for the UW was sent air mail by my aunt and uncle and finally caught up with me in Saigon. I'd only skimmed through it, never thinking I'd need to apply, but remembered that the fee for sending it in was $50. I didn't have $50. I hurried back to the ship to set up for lunch.

Two of the Ordinary Seamen, Rick Hamilton on the 12-4 watch and Malvin Jerkins on the 4-8, were 18 like me and in that year's draft lottery, but I didn't know their birthdates. The deck department broke watches in port and everyone was on day work. Both Ordinaries were at lunch that day. I told them to meet me in my fo'c'sle right after lunch, before they went back on deck and after I'd finished cleaning up the messhall.

"Here are the numbers." I had the Stars and Stripes spread out on the little desk next to my locker. Rick looked first. I don't remember exactly what number his birthday drew but it fell into the uncertain zone between 100 and 150.

"I won't get drafted," Rick said cockily.

"Well, I will unless I get into college," I responded. "I've got number 68. Do you have any scrip left? I've only got $20 MPC and I need $50 to send in an application."

Before he could answer, the 4-8 Ordinary elbowed his way in to look at the newspaper. "Ha! No chance!" I don't remember his number either but it was well over 150. I think Malvin had been on another ship before the Del Valle and might have locked into the deferment for seamen, so he probably didn't have anything to worry about.

"Why is the newspaper quoting that has-been, General Hershey," Malvin demanded to know. "He got sacked from the Selective Service last winter after the Supreme Court ruled that his order to revoke student deferments was illegal."

"What order was that?" Rick asked.

"Hershey ordered that any student demonstrating against the war would lose his student deferment and get drafted immediately. That made the students demonstrate even more. It's part of the reason for all the campus riots last year. He's one of the old farts from World War II, like the ones that are on here."

"World War II? Hell," I piped in, "he's from World War I! I read all about him in the newspaper when Nixon repealed the deferment for merchant seamen in April. Nixon loved that Hershey was messing with college students but he was a political hot potato after that Supreme Court decision, so Nixon kicked him upstairs. Hershey got promoted and is now an advisor to the president. The Stars and Stripes is probably still quoting him because Nixon made him a four star general —the only four star general who's never been in combat."

"He should be in a nursing home," Malvin added.

"That wouldn't change the lottery numbers." I turned to Rick again. "I really need another $30 to apply for college. None of the Koreans in Inchon seem to like MPC. Give me the rest of yours and I'll pay you back with greenbacks at the next draw."

"OK." Rick pulled a bunch of red money out of his pocket. As luck would have it, he had $35 MPC. "Here. Pay me back before we get to Japan."

"Thanks, Rick. I've got to go get a money order."

Running back to the Army base, I got directions to the post office.

"That MPC got replaced. It's no good anymore." A tall Spec. 5 stood behind the grated window in the base post office. He was still young enough to have pimples dotting his face.

"What do you mean?" I stood in front of the window with $50 in scrip, trying to buy a money order.

"There was a C-day last month."

"What's a C-day?"

"Change day. That's when currency gets changed to a new color. You have to change it that day or you're out of luck."

"I was in Cam Ranh Bay until the end of last month. No one told me about C-day!" My state of shock from this news was turning to anger.

"You must have left before C-day. It's unannounced and happens quick to thwart the black market and money speculators. You're lucky the MPs didn't catch you taking MPC off base."

My anger turned to nervousness and guilt as I remembered my various currency crimes. "Hey man," I said to the Specialist, "you're not going to turn me in for leaving 'Nam with MPC, are you?"

"No," he laughed, "everybody knows that MPC is a joke dreamed up by some asshole at the Pentagon who's never cleaned a rifle. We call it Monopoly money around here."

"Now what do I do?" I pondered. Out loud I said, "Well, thanks for explaining the bad news." I left the post office and walked slowly back to the Del Valle with my head hung down. "The birthday for my alias drew #228," I thought morosely. "If I'd kept working at the Wesson Oil factory under a phony name I wouldn't be in this jam."

I went into the galley at 1600 that afternoon before setting up for dinner. The Third Cook was washing some collard greens in the large work sink on the port side. "Hey Harry, I need a big favor."

"What?" He looked at me suspiciously.

"I need to borrow $50 to apply for college so I don't get drafted."

"What makes you think I got $50? And if I did have $50, what makes you think I'd lend it to you?"

"Harry, I'm desperate! My birthday got #68 in the draft lottery. I'll be drafted for sure if I don't get a student deferment." The Third Cook was 26 years old and no longer had to worry about being drafted. "I'm begging you!"

"Let's say I got $50, and let's just say I lent it to you. How you going to pay me back? You already owe your soul to that Poker Book."

"I will, Harry. I swear! I won't go ashore in Japan and give you everything from the next draw that I don't have to pay the Poker Book. If that's not enough I'll make up the rest at pay-off when we get back to the States."

"You get your money at the pay-off and I might never see you again."

"I've got to try to get a student deferment, Harry. You saw what was going on in Viet Nam. What are we fighting for back there? I'm not a pacifist but I don't want to get killed for no reason! And I sure as hell don't want to get killed to help Nixon win the next election!"

Harry looked at me for a long time. "OK," he finally said. "Come to my fo'c'sle after dinner and I'll give you $50."

"Thank you! Thank you! Thank you!" I almost danced back to the messhall.

Serving dinner that evening, I noticed that Jimmy Johnson, the poker-playing 4-8 AB, had a huge black eye on the right side of his face.

After I cleaned up the messhall from dinner, I got $50 in greenbacks from the Third Cook and then retired to my own fo'c'sle. Instead of going ashore, I sat at my little desk and filled out the application for the University of Washington. "My grades suck," I said to myself while answering questions about my academic achievements. My aunt and uncle had included a transcript of grades from high school showing a grade point average of 2.5, just barely a B-. "I'm not going to get accepted with that GPA," I sighed, "but I've got to try." I climbed up to my bunk and read my book until I fell asleep.

"Where'd Jimmy Johnson get that shiner," I asked Jimmie Singleton. The 8-12 AB was the first one in for breakfast the next morning.

"Me, Ruffner, and Jimmy Johnson went to the EM Club on base the first night we got here. Jimmy was sitting at the bar next to a Negro Sergeant. He said 'nigger' a little too loud. The Sergeant gave him a roundhouse good enough to knock him off the barstool. There were both white and Negro GIs in the club, in separate groups. I thought there was going to be a race riot! Ruffner and me grabbed Jimmy and hustled him out of there fast!"

"Wow! When are we sailing for Japan?"

"We're almost finished with cargo. Probably just after lunch. Give me two eggs over easy, grits, and toast."

I used my break between breakfast and lunch to run to the base post office again. The same Spec. 5 from the day before sold me a $50 money order. I stuffed the money order into the envelope with the application to the UW. I had already begged stamps from the Judge in my fo'c'sle.

"Is this enough postage to go air mail?" I asked the Specialist.

"No," he said, "but everything from Korea except packages goes air mail to the States."

I thanked him again and went back to the ship. It was July 3rd.

Just after I finished lunch that afternoon, the deck department cast off and the S.S. Del Valle steamed for Yokohama.

It would take us four days to reach our next port. The day we left Inchon the 2nd Electrician got logged again for being too drunk to turn to.

"Why will it take us four days to get to Yokohama," I asked Jimmie Singleton the next morning. "I thought Korea and Japan were right next to each other." As usual, the 8-12 AB was my first customer for breakfast. Even though it was the 4th of July, nothing was different except that Jimmie and I were both getting paid overtime to do what we did every other day.

"They look like they're right next to each other on a map," he explained, "but we're going from the west coast of Korea to the east coast of Japan. We're still in the Yellow Sea now. We have to sail around the south end of Korea into the East China Sea. Then we dip into the Philippine Sea to get around the southern tip of Japan, and after that we have to follow the Japanese coast half-way up until we fetch Yokohama."

Jimmie looked at the menu. "I see Korean pears on here." I nodded. We'd taken on fresh stores in Inchon. "Gimme one of those plus my usual." I went to the galley to place the AB's order.

In the saloon, the Judge was covering for the Messman, Greenwalt, who was still in his rack claiming injury. Under the SIU contract, covering for an injured crewmember entitled the man doing his work to overtime so the Judge got $2.73 an hour—the same rate as me for OT. If a vessel left port short-handed, by contrast, those covering the work got only the base wages for the missing rating. The Judge likely couldn't care less about the extra OT, but I never heard him complain about the extra work.

Starting when we were in Inchon, I felt a burning sensation whenever I took a piss. It got worse and started to sting pretty bad. I asked the Third Cook about it a couple of days before we reached Yokohama. "You didn't get no rubbers from the slop chest before you went up the street in Manila, did you?" Harry asked. I shook my head. "You got the clap, John."

The Old Man put out a draw on July 6th. $75 was the most I could get. After paying half to the Poker Book and the other half to the Third Cook, I still owed Harry $12.50. I had nothing left for going ashore in Japan.

The S.S. Del Valle arrived at Yokohama on July 7th. We tied up at a large U.S. Navy base. Yokohama is close to Tokyo and is the second largest city in Japan.

The first afternoon we were there I went ashore and got a shot of penicillin at a Navy medical clinic. The Saloon Messman, Greenwalt, was taken off, too and transported to the base hospital for left leg and hip injuries. He never came back to the ship and I assume was evacuated to the U.S. for treatment. Greenwalt likely made the same amount of money I'd made so far that trip—a little more than $800/ month before taxes, including the war bonus and overtime. He must have drawn to the maximum like I had because, after deductions for the slop chest and other withholdings, his payoff in Yokohama was only $83.40. I started getting nervous after Greenwalt showed me his pay voucher. The voyage wasn't going to last much longer and I couldn't expect to net a lot more than the Saloon Messman did. "Even if I get accepted, how long will I last at the UW with $83?" I thought. The little money I had in a savings account in New Orleans would likely get eaten up by tuition and books; there wasn't going to be enough for rent and food.

My friend Rick Hamilton, the 12-4 Ordinary, knew about my financial straits and felt sorry for me. He had no intention—nor any desire—to go to college. He did have a desire to check out the nightlife in Yokohama and asked me to go with him. "C'mon man, let's go ashore! I'll buy you a drink." I didn't need persuading.

"This place is cheap!" Rick exclaimed as we walked around Yokohama that night. He got 360 yen to the dollar when he changed his money. "I'll bet you could take a $20 bill here and walk around with it for a week." Prostitutes were not out in the open like in previous ports. That was fine with me because my dick was still burning. "Let's go in here," Rick said. He and I were in front of a nightclub where well-dressed Japanese, including a lot of beautiful women with escorts, were walking in and out. We entered a doorway covered by a canopy.

"Japanese only! Japanese only!" The man screaming at us inside the entrance looked like a sumo wrestler. He didn't physically throw us out of the nightclub—he didn't have to—but we definitely got the bum's rush. I can't remember what Rick did the rest of that evening, but I went back to the ship.

The SIU had a hiring hall in Yokohama. There were plenty of job opportunities for itinerant and expatriate seamen due to all the U.S.-flagged merchant ships supplying the military in Japan, Korea, and Viet Nam. On July 8th Charles Klaser signed on as O.S.-Maintenance (Ordinary Seaman on the day watch), replacing the regular Day Man, Robert Birmingham, the AB-Maintenance, who'd been flown home from Saigon with a broken ankle. No Saloon Messman was dispatched from the union hall to replace Greenwalt. I don't know why not—maybe no one wanted the job. That meant the Judge would no longer get overtime for the rest of the voyage, doing Greenwalt's job as well as his own BR duties, just the Saloon Messman's base wage of $12.15/day.

That same day we shifted the ship from Yokohama to another U.S. Navy base, about 20 miles away at Yokosuka. Yokosuka was at the entrance to Tokyo Bay from the Pacific Ocean. We were only there one day and I didn't go ashore. "You didn't miss anything," Jimmie Singleton told me at breakfast. "Navy squid wreck it for us everywhere they go. There's too many of them and they pay too much for everything, driving up prices." Jimmie also told me that battleships and aircraft carriers for the Imperial Japanese Navy were built at Yokosuka before World War II, after which the U.S. Navy took over. It was now home port for the U.S. Seventh Fleet, chief source of naval support for the Viet Nam war.

The next day, July 9th, we cast off and steamed for San Francisco.

It would take us less than two weeks, steaming across the Pacific, to fetch San Francisco from Japan. Going the other way, from Panama to Saigon, had taken a month. Jimmie Singleton explained to me that the Earth was shaped like an egg—larger around the middle—and that's why it took less time to go across the North Pacific than it did to go across the South Pacific near the equator, even though the distances looked the same on a map.

The day after I got a shot of penicillin in Yokohama, it didn't hurt anymore to take a piss. Two days after we left Yokosuka though, there was burning again. The clap was back! In Viet Nam, I'd heard rumors from GIs that the Viet Cong were deliberately infecting prostitutes with incurable strains of venereal disease—they called it Vietnam Rose—to give to American soldiers.

I leaned over the rail on the fantail that evening after supper, smoking a cigarette, and took stock of the situation. I'd fled to New Orleans from the Maine detective, who probably didn't have enough evidence to arrest me. I'd joined the merchant marine to get a draft deferment after the draft deferment for seamen had been repealed. I'd wanted a draft deferment in the first place to stay away from Viet Nam, and the ship I was put on went to Viet Nam. Once on the ship, I'd lost almost all of my base wages gambling. I probably wouldn't get accepted by the University of Washington, so I'd be drafted and sent back to Viet Nam. If I did get accepted and got a student deferment, I didn't have enough money to stay in the UW and would soon lose my student deferment, be drafted and sent back to Viet Nam. If I hadn't stupidly worn out my welcome at the factory in New Orleans I could have kept my alias, drawn #228 in the draft lottery, and wouldn't have to worry about a deferment. The only women I'd slept with were prostitutes, and one of them gave me a lethal dose. If I didn't get shot in Viet Nam, I'd die slowly from incurable gonorrhea. "I'm only 18 and have already totally fucked up the rest of my life!" Thoughts about throwing myself over the rail crossed my mind, but again I remembered that I didn't have the courage to commit suicide. So, instead of jumping into the Pacific Ocean, I went back to my fo'c'sle to read a book.

On July 14th we crossed the dateline and worked the same date twice, two days of work for one day of pay. My Pantryman and I alternated on making the cold drinks, without incident, even though there were two even days in a row.

On July 16th, the Old Man put out a draw. I'm not sure why he did that in the middle of the Pacific Ocean. We were less than a week away from the States, where we'd be paid off. I wondered if it had something to do with the Poker Book. I got $75. That was enough to finally pay off the Poker Book, give the Third Cook the $12.50 that I still owed, and leave me with $20.

On July 17th, the 2nd Electrician got logged again for staying in his rack, drunk, instead of working. I wondered how he had rationed himself to still have some booze left better than a week after leaving Yokosuka.

The nightly poker game had fizzled out somewhere between Cam Ranh Bay and Inchon. After all the suckers in the crew got fleeced, the sharks started devouring their own. Even Ruffner, one of the 12-4 ABs, dropped out. Jimmy Johnson and Benny Brinson the Bo's'n by themselves weren't enough to play poker, so the game stopped. To fill the void in the messhall after dinner, Ruffner introduced the game of Bouré right after the Old Man put out a draw.

Bouré, pronounced boo-ray, is a Cajun game played in Louisiana. I'd heard about it when I lived in New Orleans from black longshoremen who played it on the riverfront. The game is a cross between Bridge and poker with a pot that can get wilder than seven-card stud. Five cards are dealt to each player, face-down, like in draw poker. Then five tricks are taken, like in Bridge—also like in Hearts or the similar game of Spades—with Aces high and a trump suit determined when the dealer turns over the next card after finishing the deal. The pot is taken by the player winning the most tricks during each hand or split between winning players if there's a tie. Any player who doesn't win a single trick—and there can be more than one player who doesn't—has to match the pot for the next round.

Two to seven people can play. The first night, at 1830 when the game began at the large corner table in the messhall, Ruffner had enticed both his watch partners into playing—my pal Rick, the 12-4 Ordinary, and James Bast, the other 12-4 AB. In his 50s with a pot belly, Bast was one of the 'WWII old farts' that Malvin kept railing about. The new O.S. Day Man, Charles Klaser, was also at the table. He was clean-cut and looked to be in his late 20s, didn't hang out on the fantail, and I don't remember him talking much during the two weeks he was on the Del Valle. The fifth seat was taken by Philip, Jimmy Johnson's watch partner, who apparently was looking to make up for the drubbing he'd taken in the poker game. Philip was on the 4-8 watch, playing while on Standby and wouldn't be there long before he had to relieve the Lookout. The last of six seats was occupied by the Baker.

I stood behind Rick and watched the game until I felt confident about the rules. Everyone threw in a 25-cent ante and then looked at the cards they were dealt. At that point you could fold, but if you didn't fold you were committed and risked matching the pot if you failed to win at least one trick. Those who stayed in had to ante another quarter and could discard up to all five cards in their hand. I liked this game. Unlike poker, one couldn't be bet out of the running. If the pot was too rich for your blood, you simply didn't ante again after looking at your cards, because you knew in advance how much you were betting. I took Philip's seat when he got up to relieve Malvin, the 4-8 Ordinary, standing Lookout on the bow.

As a child I'd been taught to play Whist by my grandmother and Bridge by my father. After that I played countless games of cut-throat Hearts with my sisters, and in high school I played Spades for money. I was good at trick games. And I was good at Bouré. I prospered over the course of a dozen hands, slowly but consistently, and doubled the $20 I'd started with.

When Philip relieved Malvin on the bow and took over as Lookout, Malvin in turn had gone to the bridge to relieve the other 4-8 AB, Jimmy Johnson, at the wheel and took over steering the ship. Jimmy Johnson was now on Standby. He came down to the messhall to make a fresh pot of coffee before calling the 8-12 watch in both deck and engine departments. There was a sneer on his face and when he walked behind Ruffner's chair. I heard part of his comment about "coon-ass cards." The last traces of a huge shiner were still visible around Jimmy Johnson's right eye.

The game broke up at 2200 hours. I had over $50 when it did.

Bouré continued the next night. Rick and Bast hadn't done so well and dropped out. Their chairs were taken by the two Pantrymen, Paul and Louis. I played cautiously, never staying in a hand when not certain that I could take at least one trick, so I wouldn't get bouréd. The new Day Man, Charles, wasn't as cautious. He got dollar signs in his eyes when the pot was up to $50 one time and he stayed in when he shouldn't have. Ruffner and the Baker got two tricks each and split the pot. My Pantryman and I both folded before the second ante. Louis got one trick and barely saved himself. Charles didn't take a trick and was bouréd. He had to match the $50 pot and put it into the middle of the table for the next hand. That was about all the money he had in front of him and it looked like he'd lost his stomach for the game. He stood up and left the table. Ruffner won the $50-plus pot the next hand. No one got bouréd so we started over again with six quarters in the middle of the table.

72

Jimmie Singleton took the Day Man's chair briefly, before going on watch at 1945 hours. He was replaced by Clarence Reney, the 12-4 Fireman. Clarence reminded me of Elmer Fudd from the Bugs Bunny cartoon. Balding and with a paunch, pale white skin, and not much muscle, the 12-4 Fireman fit right into the 4-8 Ordinary's category of 'W.W.II old farts.' I could tell by the way Clarence handled his cards that he was no stranger to gambling.

By the time the second night of Bouré was over I had better than $70.

And so it went on the next two nights, July 18th and 19th, with shifting players. My winnings slowly increased. The night after that, July 20th, was the eve of our arrival in San Francisco and the end of the voyage. There was a certain electricity in the air around the Bouré table. All seated knew that this was their last chance. Most of the early players were still there: Ruffner and the Baker, the two Pantrymen, Clarence the 12-4 Fireman, and me. By that time I had slightly more than $100 in front of me.

The betting got more reckless than usual, and there were several bourés, sometimes more than one in the same hand. That drove the pot up quickly and soon there was close to $90 in the middle of the table. Not everyone had $90 to stay in the next hand, although I suppose that if one of the players had a pat hand they'd quickly run to their locker or try to get an emergency loan from one of the half-dozen spectators. This was serious business.

It was Louis the Saloon Pantryman's turn to deal. After five cards had been dealt to all six players, Louis turned over a 4 of diamonds. "Hot shit!" I thought. I had three high trump cards—an ace, jack and 10 of diamonds. My other two cards were an ace of clubs and a 10 of spades. "I'm going to win this hand for sure!

The Baker was to the dealer's left and first to announce. "Fold." The 12-4 Fireman, Clarence, threw his cards in, too.

"I'm in." I tossed a quarter into the pot.

"Me too," said my Pantryman, Paul. I looked at the pile of money in front of him. He had $90, in case he got bouréd, but just barely. I figured that he must have a real good hand to take that kind of risk, or maybe he thought that the odds of taking at least one trick were acceptable after the Baker and the Fireman dropped out. Ruffner stayed in, too. He had a lot more than $90 in front of him

"I'm not staying in this game!" Louis threw his cards into the middle of the table. He didn't have $90 in front of him and it was now down to me, my Pantryman, and Ruffner.

I discarded first, throwing away only my 10 of spades, which was replaced with a jack of hearts. My Pantryman also discarded only one card, and likely had a strong hand. Ruffner, looking a bit nervous, took three cards.

Being left of the dealer, I played the first card. Under the rules, I had to lead with my highest trump card if I had a queen or higher. I put down my ace of diamonds, a card that was impossible to beat and assured me of at least one trick. It was my Pantryman's turn. He had to follow suit but didn't have to play his highest card if he couldn't beat what was already on the table. Paul laid down a 2 of diamonds. Ruffner played a queen of diamonds. That meant he was out of trump cards—because I had the jack and 10 of diamonds—unless he had the king. I won the first trick.

"I'll find out real quick if Ruffner's got the king," I thought as I started the next trick with a jack of diamonds. Paul followed suit with a 5, but Ruffner played a 3 of clubs instead. He was out of trump cards! I won that trick too.

I next led with my last trump card, the 10 of diamonds. Paul played a 6 of diamonds. "Damn!" I thought. "If he's got any more trump cards I won't be able to boure' his ass." Ruffner played a 3 of spades. I won trick number three. That meant, out of five possible tricks, I'd already won the $90 pot. "The challenge now," I gloated, "is to see who I can bouré."

I led the fourth trick with an ace of clubs. Paul played the jack of clubs and Ruffner a 5 of spades because he couldn't follow suit. I won trick number four.

My last card was a jack of hearts. The rule was that one had to follow suit. There were no more trumps left, so hearts higher than a jack were the only cards that could beat me. My Pantryman played a king of clubs. Ruffner looked pained as he laid down an ace of spades. I'd won all five tricks. Ruffner and my Pantryman were bouréd!

Two bourés meant there was over $180 in the pot for the next hand. It was the Baker's turn to deal, and diamonds were trump again. I had a good hand. My only trump card was the king but I figured that was high enough to get me at least one trick so I wouldn't get bouréd.

Clarence the Fireman folded right away as did, in turn, the Saloon Pantryman and the Baker. My Pantryman, Paul, wanted to stay in the game but couldn't match the pot with the little bit of money he had in front of him. There was a short break in the game while he ran to his locker and came back with $200. It looked like a rematch between me, Paul, and Ruffner.

After discarding two cards, I lucked out and was dealt trump cards in exchange, the jack and 5 of diamonds. Ruffner and I took two tricks each that hand and split the pot—raking in better than $90 each. Paul got one trick so he didn't have to match the pot again.

It was close to 2200 hours. After all that excitement, there was little interest in starting another pot build-up and the game broke up. I'd won almost $300 in Bouré, about the total of what I'd lost in the poker game.

The next day, July 21st, we broke foreign articles in San Francisco.

The Old Man paid us off in cash—$100 bills. I got three of them plus some extra bills and change.

Coming aboard as soon as the gangway was lowered was an SIU Patrolman and a couple of guys from Customs. The union Patrolman sat in the messhall, collecting dues and "donations" to SPAD (Seafarers Political Activity Donation)—acting much like Jimmy Johnson with the Poker Book. Harry, the Third Cook, had warned me that, as a new guy, I was also going to have to pay up to $800 for SIU assessments back to 1948, on top of my union dues. That didn't happen. I was hit up only for two calendar quarters of regular dues and $20 to SPAD. I found out later that the president, Paul Hall, and two vice-presidents of the SIU had just been indicted by a grand jury in New York for illegal political payments and for shaking down seamen for improper "donations."

The two guys from Customs were supposed to look for drugs smuggled from Viet Nam, but I didn't see them do much. They never even came to my fo'c'sle, to say nothing of looking in my locker.

As soon as Customs cleared the ship, I grabbed a fistful of quarters from my Bouré winnings and ran down the gangway to a pay phone, to call my aunt and uncle. My Aunt Judy answered. "You got accepted to the UW, Johnny."

75

I was ecstatic and almost did a headstand in the phone booth. We caught up on news for a few minutes but the call was expensive so we kept it short. "This changes everything," I thought after hanging up. "I need to stay on this ship as long as I can." The scuttlebutt in the messhall was that the Del Valle was to run down the West Coast and then go back to Viet Nam with a load of napalm bombs. I needed to earn more money for school, and I needed more sea time to keep my B-book. The SIU Shipping Rules required 90 days per year aboard union ships to keep one's seniority. I'd only been on the Del Valle for 86 days. I decided to stay on for coastwise articles.

Almost everyone in the crew piled off as soon as they could, including my friend Rick Hamilton, the 12-4 Ordinary. I didn't toast the end of the voyage with Rick, or anybody else for that matter. It was something of a shock to be back to a place like California with a 21-year-old drinking age that was actually enforced. Everything was happening fast during our short stay in 'Frisco and there wasn't enough time to go to a hospital to get treated for the clap again. At some point a Coast Guard Lieutenant came aboard to examine the logbook for violations of the law and regulations. He never asked to talk to me, and I never heard anything more about being logged. Apparently my supposed crime of hiring a Filipino to work for me (which I hadn't done) wasn't severe enough for further action. I don't know what he did to others in the crew who'd been logged, the 2nd Electrician in particular.

On July 22nd I signed coastwise articles. That meant I could get off in any U.S. port, like San Diego or Long Beach.

One in the crew who didn't pile off in 'Frisco was Clarence, the 12-4 Fireman. I was surprised to see him at dinner the day after we got paid off. Under the SIU contract, a seaman is entitled to one day off after a foreign voyage if he commits to making another trip. The Fireman told me he took his payoff and went to Reno, Nevada on his day off to gamble. "How much money you got left, Clarence?" I asked jokingly while he looked at the menu.

"None, but I was smart."

"Smart? By losing your whole payoff?"

"Yeah. I bought a round-trip bus ticket before I left to make sure I could get back to the ship."

"Jesus, Clarence, you went to 'Nam and then blew three month's wages in Reno! Now you're broke and are going back there?"

The Fireman shrugged as if that was nothing unusual. "Gimme shit-on-a-shingle." What he ordered was creamed chipped beef on toast. The new Chief Cook didn't seem very ambitious about the menu, or maybe it was the new Steward's idea to put creamed beef on the dinner menu instead of just for breakfast.

The Del Valle had taken on a new, San Francisco crew. The Judge stayed on as BR but I don't remember any other familiar faces in the steward department during the final week I worked as Crew Messman.

The ship left San Francisco the evening of the 22nd and steamed south for San Diego. We arrived on July 24th. I made a lot of money working overtime during the seven days I was on coastwise articles. While at sea the new Steward turned me to for three hours every afternoon—1300-1600—and sometimes after dinner in the evenings to sougee the messhall, clean and arrange the storerooms and generally get the steward department spaces ready for another long voyage. In port, one got OT automatically for working before 0800 and after 1700, called "port time" in the SIU contract. That meant I got three hours of OT every weekday in port without working extra, and I still got to go ashore when I wasn't working in the afternoons helping to take on stores for even more overtime.

In San Diego I took an afternoon off and went to the Naval Hospital where merchant seamen could receive free treatment. I walked into a large reception area filled with young Navy wives and their screaming children. "No wonder they're called Navy brats," I thought as I walked up to the front counter and told a Corpsman why I was there.

"What'd you say you were here for?" the Corpsman asked after looking at the intake sheet, where I'd written "merchant seaman" in the space for rank. I told him again and he responded, "I still can't hear you."

"Venereal disease," I said loudly. The heads of 20 Navy wives swung around to look at me and I turned beet red with embarrassment.

I got shot up with some sort of newly-developed antibiotic and went back to the ship.

I don't know what cargo we loaded or off-loaded in San Diego. If I had to guess, I'd say we were there to unload household furnishings for Navy families returning from Japan. At any rate, we left late on the 26th. When I got called out of my bunk the morning of the 27th, we were already tied to the dock in Long Beach, California.

500-lb. napalm bombs were being loaded on the Del Valle when I went ashore after finishing lunch. I caught a cab and went to see the just-released movie, "MASH," with Elliott Gould and Donald Sutherland.

I quit the S.S. Del Valle on July 29, 1970 in Long Beach, just before the crew had to sign foreign articles. It was good timing. I had 90 days of sea time, as of the 26th so I could keep my B seniority in the union. After taxes, my pay-off for coastwise articles came to well over $300. The final straw was scuttlebutt in the messhall that Delta Steamship was refusing to pay the crew a 10% bonus on base wages for "explosives" because napalm, technically, wasn't defined as such in the SIU contract—even though "poison gases" and "dynamite" were. I guessed that the type of napalm being loaded—manufactured by Dow Chemical, as I was told by a long-haired Ordinary who joined the ship in 'Frisco—was developed after the latest SIU contract was negotiated. It was time to get off.

Because I'd made the foreign voyage, I would be entitled to transportation back to my port of engagement. That meant that a big part of my pay-off was an extra amount for airfare to New Orleans, because I got the cash equivalent of a first-class ticket. I needed to go back to New Orleans anyway, to get my savings from the Whitney National Bank under the name of my alias. I figured to save a whole bunch of money by hitchhiking to New Orleans instead of taking a jet plane.

Because I'd gotten more than 90 days of sea time, I would also be entitled to vacation pay after I submitted an application at the union hall in Seattle. Under the SIU contract, seamen were entitled to a vacation benefit of 12 days of base wages for every 30 days worked, once getting over the 90-day threshold. That meant that for working 93 days I could apply for about $450 in vacation pay, minus deductions. "I'm rich!" I thought. "I've got almost enough money to make it through a whole year of college until next summer when I'll catch another ship. If the money runs low, I can always work over Christmas vacation."

The first thing I did when I got off the ship was go to a bank and trade almost $700 for a money order in the same amount. Then I went to a post office and mailed it to myself at my aunt and uncle's address. I still had a little money left over to buy food during my trip to New Orleans. I bought a map and walked to the highway with my suitcase. "It still burns when I piss," I thought as I walked, "and it's been four days since I got another shot. I guess I've got the clap for good."

From California Route 1, I got a short ride to U.S. Route 6, east on U.S. 91, and then a long one north on U.S. 395 to Barstow, California. From there it was a straight shot across the Southwest on U.S. Route 66 to the Texas Panhandle without having to change direction.

It was hotter than hell in Barstow that afternoon—better than 100 degrees—and there were a lot of hitchhikers thumbing east. Hitchhiker etiquette is that you can't stand in front of the guys who got there first, and have to go farther down the road before you stick out your thumb. All the hitchhikers in Barstow trying to thumb Route 66 were under an overpass to stay in the shade; there were so many that they were two deep. It was going to be a long wait before I was first in line under the overpass. It was either thumb in the sun or wait in the shade. I walked down the road apiece, squinted into the sun—I had no sun glasses—and stuck out my thumb.

Four hours later, when the sun was going down, I was badly sunburned and still in Barstow. I felt dehydrated and a bit goofy. The few cars and trucks that had stopped picked up the hitchhikers under the bridge. Someone must have finally stopped for me but I have no memory of it. In fact I have no memory at all until three days later when I was in New Orleans. I don't think I ate or slept for those three days and guess I had sunstroke, but I must have made really good time because it's almost 2,000 miles from Long Beach to New Orleans. I don't know how I did it, but I made it there.

In New Orleans I got a cheap hotel near the Jax Brewery on Decatur Street and slept for a good long time. By the time I got up it no longer hurt to piss. The first thing I did after I got some food was go to the U.S. Public Health Service Hospital, by the river on State Street, to

79

get tested for gonorrhea. Merchant seamen got free medical care for life at USPHS facilities—formerly known as the Marine Hospitals—in port cities all over the country. The test came back negative.

"I'm clean!" I said out loud, while walking out of the hospital. I wondered if that new antibiotic in San Diego took a long time to kick in or whether the clap got burned out by sunstroke.

I stayed a couple of days in New Orleans, basically wrapping up the life of my alias and picking up mail in my real name, which was sent to Seamen's General Delivery at the main post office. I had several hundred dollars in an account at the Whitney National Bank in the name of my alias. I closed it and put all but $20 into a money order, which I again mailed to myself at my aunt and uncle's address. Then I stuck my thumb out and hitchhiked toward Seattle. It was August 3, 1970.

I was aiming for Route 66. Unlike getting to New Orleans, when I ended up on Route 66 by accident, this time I actually wanted to travel that highway all the way to the West Coast. There's no road that could be faster, I thought, than one you can hitch 2,000 miles in three days.

My first ride was from a schoolteacher in his late 20s or early 30s on summer vacation. As we drove west on U.S. Route 90, the radio blared out warnings about Hurricane Celia approaching Louisiana. The wind started picking up and soon was blowing pretty good. My ride lost his nerve, dropped me off, turned around and high-tailed it back to his house in New Orleans.

"Well," I thought as I stood by the side of the road with my battered suitcase, trying to keep my spirits up while watching panicked drivers racing to unknown destinations, "this couldn't be as bad as that typhoon I was in on the Del Valle." The wind was picking up and soon gusted so hard that I had to lean forward to not get blown over. I'd be a liar if I said I wasn't scared. There were no motels around, and even if there were I didn't want to use half my travel money to Seattle before I got out of Louisiana.

I lucked out. A semi-truck stopped less than 30 minutes later and let me jump in. The driver was hauling a load to Oklahoma City and was as eager to escape the hurricane as I was. The cops had other worries, I guess he was thinking, and the truck ignored the speed limit. We hauled ass out of Louisiana and into Texas, as the wind blew and the shit flew, doing better than 80 mph on the straight stretches.

We'd just cut north, near Houston, when we heard over the radio that Hurricane Celia made a landfall at Corpus Christi, Texas—far south of us—rather than in Louisiana. I guess Corpus Christi got hit pretty hard. The radio reported lots of death and damage.

The trucker dropped me off where Route 66 passed through Oklahoma City late that night, and I had another straight shot to the West Coast. There was no place to sleep, so I stuck out my thumb.

Over the next three days I hitchhiked around the clock on Route 66 and made good time. The only sleep I got was an occasional cat-nap in the middle of the night, in some field beside the highway, when no headlights were visible in the distance. Memories of rides across Oklahoma, Texas, New Mexico, and Arizona are a blur of black-top dreams. My memory starts to come back, a little bit, in Flagstaff, Arizona. That's probably because I got stuck there for about three hours.

There were about 40 hitchhikers ahead of me in Flagstaff, headed west on Route 66, more than I'd ever seen in one place. It wasn't unpleasant waiting to be first in line beside the road—it was only about 80 degrees—but I didn't dare sleep lest I miss a ride, even though I was very tired from not having a good night's sleep since New Orleans.

When it was finally my turn, a yellow VW beetle stopped. "Hop on in, brother!" The driver was a shuck 'n' jive black guy from Amarillo, Texas on his way to California as I found out. He wore expensive-looking sunglasses and had a large Afro haircut. A Stevie Wonder number blared out from four speakers in the little car.

"Nice tunes," I said while looking at the first eight-track tape player I'd ever seen built into the dashboard of a car.

"Music, my man!" The driver shifted the volume around to various speakers, demonstrating his total control over the direction of the sound. "It's not a luxury, it's a necessity."

That was a fun ride. The eight-track dude dropped me off in Paso Robles, California. Paso Robles is on U.S. Route 101, half way between Los Angeles and San Francisco—a great place to start my hitchhike north to Seattle.

It took the rest of the day to get even close to San Francisco. My last ride was with a hippie couple in a truck that had a homemade camper on the back. The three of us rode in the cab of the truck. It felt nice to sit thigh-to-thigh with the woman in the middle. They were going to Half Moon Bay to groove for a while. I had fantasies about sleeping in their small camper and sharing the friendly woman. It was in the middle of the night when we got to the turn-off for Half Moon Bay. I got dropped off on the shoulder of 101 before they turned off and drove toward the beach. "Damn!" I thought as I started walking. "She was really pretty."

There was hardly any traffic during the wee hours. I found a grove of trees and slept for a couple of hours until first light when the sound of cars woke me up.

It took all morning to get through the greater San Francisco area. I never had to wait too long for a ride but they were always short hops. By mid-afternoon I was standing on the shoulder of 101 just north of Novato, California in Marin County—about 30 miles beyond San Francisco.

It was hot that day and getting hotter. I was sweating and wanted to take off my shirt. Three days earlier, in Oklahoma, I'd taken off my shirt while hitchhiking. It was close to 100 degrees in the small town on Route 66 where I'd been waiting for a ride. Three teenagers picked me up—two boys and a girl, all about my age. They told me that I could get arrested for indecent exposure in that county. I didn't know if they were joking or serious, but I put my shirt back on and kept it on until I got out of Oklahoma. "But this is California." I took my shirt off. Not long afterwards a red 1966 VW Beetle stopped to pick me up. Two women in their early 20s sat in the front seats.

"Thanks," I said as I threw in my suitcase and squeezed into the back seat, pushing aside a mountain of kids' toys. Countless dolls and plastic, miniature construction vehicles made it difficult to find space. The woman in the passenger seat had blonde hair. That's about all I could see of her as I was trying to situate myself.

"You look hot!" the driver said, when I'd carved out a place to sit. "Want to go swimming?" She had brown eyes and long dark hair and could have been Sophia Loren's shorter sister.

"Sure." We drove to the Russian River close by. I bought a watermelon along the way.

Down at the swimming area they took me to, the two women took off their clothes to reveal bikinis underneath. I didn't have a swimsuit and was too embarrassed to swim in just underpants, so I took off my shoes, emptied my pockets and dove in with my blue jeans on. The water felt great!

My brown jackknife with the broken tip wasn't long enough to cut the watermelon, so I smashed it on a rock. I passed around the jagged pieces and we all buried our faces in the luscious chunks. We swam again, to wash off the watermelon, and talked while lounging in the sun. The driver's name was Laura; I don't remember much about her blonde friend. Laura was a single mother who lived in Novato. She said she wanted to check out Seattle. There was no hanky-panky that day on the Russian River—her friend was always there—but the spark between Laura and me was of high voltage.

"I've got to pick up the kids at my dad's," Laura announced in late afternoon. The swim party was over and we got back into the VW.

Laura and I exchanged addresses and phone numbers when she stopped at the entrance to the highway, where I'd be going north and she south. Both women waved goodbye and I stuck out my thumb. Back on Route 101.

It was after dark that evening when a late-model Ford Cougar pulled over to pick me up. By that time I'd made it to the redwoods, huge trees in Northern California standing on either side of the highway. The driver was a medium-sized guy in his late 30s with sandy hair. There was barely room for my suitcase in the back seat when I jumped in. "Where you headed?" he asked.

"Seattle."

"You have a driver's license?"

"Yeah."

"Then you drive." The guy pulled over on the shoulder, less than a mile after he had picked me up. I figured he was tired.

As soon as I started driving, the guy reached into the back seat and pulled up a full bottle of expensive vodka. He broke the seal and started drinking it straight, right out of the bottle. He didn't offer me any. That's a good thing because I'd had precious little sleep during the past four days and would not have handled alcohol well. Anyway, I didn't like the taste of vodka.

I don't remember the guy's name but I remember well the story he told me as we sped north on 101 through Northern California. He drank and I drove.

He worked for Boeing in Southern California. After he got laid off he caught his wife sleeping with his best friend who still had a job. "Yesterday I said, 'Fuck all of you!'—my wife, my house, and my so-called friend—and left. This morning I put what I needed into the car and hit the road!"

"Where are you going?" I wondered silently how this guy could have fit a whole lifetime into the trunk and backseat of a Cougar.

"Anywhere! Nowhere! Who cares?" My ride-host was starting to get drunk. "I've got some relatives near Everett, Washington. Maybe I'll go there for a little while."

"What are you going to do next?"

"Go back and kill my wife? Go back and kill Don, who I thought was my friend? I don't know. Maybe go lay on a beach or join a monastery. I've got a Colt .38 revolver and a Smith & Wesson .40-caliber semi-automatic in the backseat, and a shotgun in the trunk. I can do anything I want!"

He passed out somewhere south of Crescent City, before we crossed the state line into Oregon. The bottle of vodka was still about one-quarter full. I kept driving.

I don't know where it was on the southern Oregon coast that I fell asleep. As near as I can figure, the highway curved to the right and I went straight. When I opened my eyes, the Cougar was doing 50 miles-per-hour in a hotel parking lot headed straight toward double glass doors at the main entrance barely 200 feet in front of me! Lucky for me the Cougar had new tires and good brakes. It came to a smoking stop less than ten feet away from three front steps to the glass doors. There was a long patch of 'scratch' across the parking lot and the air was rank with the smell of burnt rubber. The owner of the Cougar never even woke up.

I restarted the stalled car and drove back onto 101 from the hotel parking lot. I pulled over at the first wide shoulder and napped behind the wheel. Waking at first light from the sound of traffic, a couple of hours later, I pushed north up the Oregon coast.

In contrast to California, the coast of Oregon was completely undeveloped. There were lots of Winnebagos and other vacationers' vehicles slowing traffic, so at Newport I exited off 101 to go east to the new Interstate 5. The owner of the Cougar woke up soon after. "Where are we?" He rubbed his eyes.

"U.S. Route 20 in Oregon," I replied, "headed for I-5 so we can make time." He didn't say anything.

I drove up I-5 at 75 mph—just over the speed limit—through Oregon and into Washington. The owner of the Cougar surprisingly had no apparent hangover. He nipped at the vodka bottle that morning but didn't get drunk.

Following the Columbia River to Kelso, Washington, about 125 miles south of Seattle, I exited the freeway and stopped for burgers at a Dairy Queen. We ordered our food to go. Back in the Cougar—with me behind the wheel in the Dairy Queen parking lot—the owner of the car said: "Let's rob this joint." He motioned his head toward the backseat where the two pistols were.

His request was quite shocking. But I was seriously sleep-deprived and more than a little road-crazy. I pondered this idea for about 10 seconds and decided that it wasn't unreasonable, given the poor service we'd gotten at the counter. "OK," I responded.

He started to reach into the backseat but then hesitated, looking at me. I was an 18-year-old hitchhiker of whom he knew nothing. Looking at his eyes I could almost hear him thinking: "This punk might take my guns and my car, shoot me and then take off." "No, we can't do it," he said out loud. I was relieved and wondered why I'd ever agreed to armed robbery in the first place. I drove back onto I-5.

I took the Cougar right to my aunt and uncle's house before getting out and saying goodbye to my new friend.

Back in Seattle by mid-August, I went to Schmitz Hall to enroll as a freshman at the University of Washington. I signed up for three classes—math, chemistry, and a political science course called Modern Government—totaling 14 academic credits.

At $144 per academic quarter, tuition at the UW was a lot cheaper than I expected. With pockets jingling after cashing the money orders I'd mailed to myself, I rented a studio apartment on Capitol Hill for $90/month. Near Volunteer Park on 15th Avenue East, the apartment was about three miles from campus. Then I splurged and paid $870 for a 1968 Norton P-11 motorcycle, purchased at Poke's Cycle on 12th Avenue. The P-11 was a dirt racer with high exhaust pipes, a bastard child of the recent merger between the Matchless and Norton motorcycle companies in England. It was so fast that when I twisted the throttle it felt like I would become airborne. Sometimes it was difficult to hang on to the handlebars. I figured that a P-11 would get me to class on time!

After I registered at the UW I went to check in with my draft board. Miss Craig from Local Board #6 fussed and fuddled with my UW registration papers before finally confirming my II-S draft deferment. "If you hadn't started college, young man, you would have been inducted this October." I thanked her and ran to the elevator. Back on 1st Avenue, I jumped on my Norton and happily sped away from the Federal Building.

Classes for Autumn Quarter at the UW started on September 22, 1970, the day after I turned 19.

EPILOGUE

I never saw any of my shipmates from the S.S. Del Valle again. I exchanged a few letters with Rick Hamilton, the 12-4 Ordinary. He got drafted. Rick didn't last long in the Army and went AWOL from Fort Polk, Louisiana during Basic Training. The last time I heard from him he was in California, on the run from the FBI.

I did OK at the UW during Autumn Quarter. Over Christmas vacation I caught a job as Saloon Pantryman aboard the S.S. Walter Rice, at Longview, Washington on the Columbia River. The ship was bound for Corpus Christi, Texas to pick up aluminum ore to be brought back to the Reynolds Metals plant in Longview. That's another story. Suffice it to say that I didn't get back to Seattle until two weeks after classes started for Winter Quarter, and my grades started slipping below the grade point average required to keep my II-S deferment.

I never heard from the Maine detective again.